# Java® Essentials

## by Doug Lowe and Paul McFedries

for **dummies®**

A Wiley Brand

# Java® Essentials For Dummies®

Published by: **John Wiley & Sons, Inc.**, 111 River Street, Hoboken, NJ 07030-5774, www.wiley.com

For general information on our other products and services, please contact our Customer Care Department within the U.S. at 877-762-2974, outside the U.S. at 317-572-3993, or fax 317-572-4002. For technical support, please visit https://hub.wiley.com/community/support/dummies.

Wiley publishes in a variety of print and electronic formats and by print-on-demand. Some material included with standard print versions of this book may not be included in e-books or in print-on-demand. If this book refers to media such as a CD or DVD that is not included in the version you purchased, you may download this material at http://booksupport.wiley.com. For more information about Wiley products, visit www.wiley.com.

Library of Congress Control Number: 2024944840

ISBN 978-1-394-29697-2 (pbk); ISBN 978-1-394-29699-6 (ebk); ISBN 978-1-394-29698-9 (ebk)

SKY10090205_110624

# Contents at a Glance

# Table of Contents

# Introduction

Welcome to *Java Essentials For Dummies*. This book contains all the basic information you need to know to get going with Java programming, starting with writing statements and using variables and ending with techniques for using Java features such as arrays. Along the way, you find plenty of not-so-basic information about working with classes and objects, handling exceptions, and working from the command line.

The basic idea here is that we've tried to wring out the not-quite-200-or-so most useful pages of information on the most important Java programming topics: setup and configuration, basic programming, and object-oriented programming. Thus, you get a nice, trim book with just the Java you need to know.

So, whether you're just getting started with Java programming or you're a seasoned pro, you've found the right book.

## About This Book

In *Java Essentials For Dummies*, all the information you need is conveniently packaged for you in-between one set of covers. And all the information is current for a recent release of Java, known as JDK 19. This book doesn't pretend to be a comprehensive reference for every detail on every possible topic related to Java programming. Instead, it shows you how to get up and running fast so that you have more time to do the things you really want to do. Designed using the easy-to-follow *For Dummies* format, this book helps you get the information you need without laboring to find it.

## Foolish Assumptions

We've never met, so it's difficult for us to make any assumptions about why you're interested in this book. However, let's start with a few basic assumptions:

>> **You own or have access to a relatively modern computer.**
The examples were created on a Windows computer, but you can learn to program in Java just as easily on a Mac or Linux computer.

>> **You're an experienced computer user.** In other words, we assume that you know the basics of using your computer, such as starting programs and working with the file system.

>> **You're interested in learning how to write programs in the Java language.** That's what this book is about, so it's a fair assumption.

We do *not* assume you have any previous programming experience in Java or in any other programming language.

# Icons Used in This Book

Like any *For Dummies* book, this book is chock-full of helpful icons that draw your attention to items of particular importance. You find the following icons throughout this book:

Danger, Will Robinson! This icon highlights information that may help you avert disaster.

WARNING

Did we tell you about the memory course we took?

REMEMBER

Pay special attention to this icon; it lets you know that some particularly useful tidbit is at hand.

TIP

# Where to Go from Here

This isn't the kind of book you pick up and read from start to finish, as if it were a cheap novel. If we ever see you reading it at the beach, we'll kick sand in your face. Beaches are for reading romance novels or murder mysteries, not programming books. Although you could read straight through from start to finish, this book is the kind you can pick up, open to just about any page, and start reading. You don't have to memorize anything in this book. It's a "need-to-know" book: You pick it up when you need to know something. Need a reminder on how to declare a class? Pick up the book. Can't remember the goofy syntax of the for loop? Pick up the book. After you find what you need, put the book down and get on with your life.

# Chapter **1**

# Installing and Using Java Tools

J ava development environments have two basic approaches. On the one hand, you can use a sophisticated integrated development environment (IDE) such as NetBeans or Eclipse. These tools combine a full-featured source editor that lets you edit your Java program files with integrated development tools, including visual development tools that let you create applications by dragging and dropping visual components onto a design surface.

At the other extreme, you can use just the basic command-line tools that are available free from Oracle's Java website (https:// java.oracle.com). Then you can use any text editor you want to create the text files that contain your Java programs (called *source files*), and compile and run your programs by typing commands at a command prompt.

**TIP**

As a compromise, you may want to use a simple development environment, such as TextPad. TextPad is an inexpensive text editor that provides some nice features for editing Java programs (such as automatic indentation) and shortcuts for compiling and running programs. It doesn't generate any code for you or provide any type of visual design aids, however. TextPad is the tool we used to develop all the examples shown in this book. For information about downloading and using TextPad, see Chapter 2.

**TIP**

If you prefer a free alternative, you can also investigate Notepad++ at https://notepad-plus-plus.org.

You can also compile and run simple Java programs online at sites such as JDoodle (www.jdoodle.com/online-java-compiler) or Programiz (www.programiz.com/java-programming/online-compiler). At these sites, you can enter simple Java programs, compile them, and run them. They're a great way to dip your toes into the shallow end of the Java programming pool without having to install anything.

# Downloading and Installing the Java Development Kit

Before you can start writing Java programs, you have to download and install the correct version of the Java Development Kit (JDK) for the computer system you're using. Oracle's Java website provides versions for Windows, macOS, and Unix. The following sections show you how to download and install the JDK.

**TIP**

If you prefer, you can download and install the open-source version of Java from https://openjdk.org.

## Downloading the JDK

To get to the download page, point your browser to www.oracle.com/java/technologies. Then follow the appropriate links to download the latest version of Java SE for your operating system. (At the time we wrote this, the latest version was 18.0.1.1. However, Java 19 was available in early release form. By the time this book hits the shelves, Java 19 or later should be available from www.oracle.com/java/technologies.)

When you get to the Java download page, you'll need to select your operating system; Java is available for Linux, macOS, and Windows. In this chapter, we show you how to deploy Java to a Windows 10 or 11 computer. The procedures for deploying Java to Linux or macOS are similar.

The JDK download comes in three versions: a compressed .zip file, an executable installer (.exe), or a Windows installer package (.msi). All are about the same size (under 200MB). We find it easier to download and run the .exe installer.

# Installing the JDK

After you download the JDK file, you can install it by running the executable file you downloaded. The procedure varies slightly depending on your operating system, but basically, you just run the JDK installation program file after you download it, as follows:

>> On a Windows system, open the folder in which you saved the installation program and double-click the installation program's icon.

>> On a Linux or macOS system, use console commands to change to the directory to which you downloaded the file and then run the program.

After you start the installation program, it prompts you for any information that it needs to install the JDK properly, such as which features you want to install and what folder you want to install the JDK in. You can safely choose the default answer for each option.

## Perusing the JDK folders

When the JDK installs itself, it creates several folders on your hard drive. The locations of these folders vary depending on your system and how you installed Java. The three most likely places to find the Java home folder in Windows are the root of your C: drive, the folder C:\Program Files\Java, or the folder C:\Program Files (x86)\Java. Within one of these locations, you'll find the Java home folder, whose name starts with jfk- and ends with the version number. For version 19, the home folder is named jdk-19.

Table 1-1 lists the subfolders created in the JDK home folder. As you work with Java, you'll refer to these folders frequently.

**TABLE 1-1** Subfolders of the JDK Home Folder

| Folder | Description |
| --- | --- |
| bin | The compiler and other Java development tools |
| conf | Configuration file |
| include | This library contains files needed to integrate Java with programs written in other languages |

**TABLE 1-1** *(continued)*

| Folder | Description |
|--------|-------------|
| jmods | Modules for the Java Module System |
| legal | Copyright and license information for various Java components |
| lib | Library files, including the Java API class library |

## Setting the JAVA_HOME and path variables

After you install the JDK, you need to configure your operating system so that it can find the JDK command-line tools. To do that, you must set two environment variables: JAVA_HOME, which provides the location of the Java home folder, and Path, which lists the folders that the operating system uses to locate executable programs. Follow these steps:

**1.** **Open File Explorer, right-click This PC, and choose Properties.**

This brings up the System Properties page.

**2.** **Click the Advanced System Settings link.**

**3.** **Click the Environment Variables button.**

The Environment Variables dialog box appears, as shown in Figure 1-1.

**4.** **In the System Variables list, click the New button.**

The New System Variable dialog box, shown in Figure 1-2, appears.

**5.** **Type** JAVA_HOME **in the Variable Name text box.**

**6.** **Click the Browse Directory button, browse to the Java home folder, and then click OK.**

This action inserts the path to the home folder in the Variable Value text box.

**7.** **Click OK.**

The JAVA_HOME variable is created.

**8.** **Scroll to the Path variable in the System Variables list, select it, and then click the Edit button.**

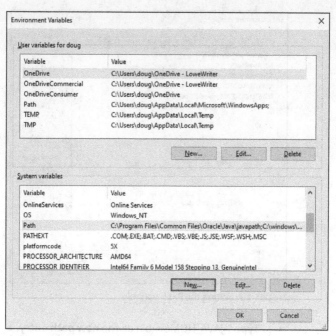

**FIGURE 1-1:** The Environment Variables dialog box.

**New System Variable**

Variable name:

Variable value:

Browse Directory...     Browse File...          OK     Cancel

**FIGURE 1-2:** Creating the JAVA_HOME variable.

This brings up a handy dialog box that lets you add or remove paths to the Path variable or change the order of the paths, shown in Figure 1-3.

**9.** **Peruse the list of entries in the** Path **variable. If you find one that references a previous version of Java, delete it.**

Specifically, look for an entry that begins with C:\Program Files\Java. If you find such an entry, select it and then click Delete.

**10.** **Click the New button.**

This opens a line for you to create a new path entry.

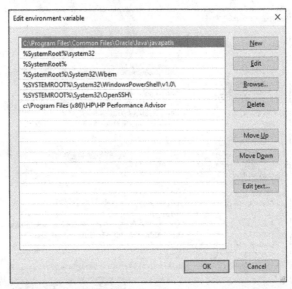

FIGURE 1-3: Editing the Path variable.

**11.** Type %JAVA_HOME%\bin **as the new path entry.**

The percent signs insert the value of the JAVA_HOME variable in your new path entry. For example, if JAVA_HOME is set to C:\Program Files\Java\jdk19, the new path entry will be C:\Program Files\Java\jdk19\bin.

**12.** **Click OK three times to exit.**

The first OK gets you back to the Environment Variables dialog box; the second OK gets you back to the System Properties dialog box; and the third OK closes the System Properties dialog box.

For Linux, the procedure depends on which shell you're using. For more information, consult the documentation for the shell you're using.

## Confirming Your Java Version

After you've installed Java, it's a good idea to confirm that you've installed the correct version. To do that, follow these steps:

1. **Press the Windows key, type** cmd, **and press Enter to open a command prompt.**

2. **Type** java -version **and press Enter.**

   This command instructs Java to display its version number. You'll see output similar to this:

   ```
   openjdk version "19-ea" 222-09-20
   OpenJDK Runtime Environment (build 19-ea+27-2074)
   OpenJDK 64-Bit Server VM (build 19-ea+27-2074, mixed
       mode, sharing)
   ```

3. **Confirm that the first line of the output reflects the version you installed.**

   In this example, Java version 19-ea is installed. The ea indicates that we're using the early-access version of Java 19, which is the version we used as we wrote this book. By the time you read this, you'll see a slightly different version of Java 19 or later. Or, you may see a Java 18 or even a Java 17 version number. Any of these versions will work for the coding examples in this book, unless we specifically mention that a specific Java version is required.

4. **Close the command window.**

# Chapter **2**

# Working with TextPad

extPad is an inexpensive ($27) text editor that you can inte-
grate with the Java Development Kit (JDK) to simplify the
task of coding, compiling, and running Java programs. It
isn't a true integrated development environment (IDE), as it lacks
features such as integrated debugging, code generators, and
drag-and-drop tools for creating graphical user interfaces.

TextPad is a popular tool for developing Java programs because
of its simplicity and speed. It's ideal for learning Java because it
doesn't generate any code for you. Writing every line of code yourself may seem like a bother, but the exercise pays off in the long
run because you have a better understanding of how Java works.

## Downloading and Installing TextPad

You can download a free evaluation version of TextPad from Helios
Software Systems at www.textpad.com. You can use the evaluation version free of charge, but if you decide to keep the program,
you must pay for it. (Helios accepts credit card payment online.)

If the Java JDK is already installed on your computer when you
install TextPad, TextPad automatically configures itself to compile and run Java programs. If you install the JDK after you install

TextPad, you need to configure TextPad for Java by following these steps:

1. **Choose Configure ⇨ Preferences to open the Preferences dialog box.**

2. **Click Tools in the tree that appears on the left side of the dialog box.**

3. **Click the Add button to reveal a drop-down list of options and then click Java SDK Commands.**

4. **Click OK.**

   The commands you need to compile and run Java programs are added to TextPad's Tools menu.

Figure 2-1 shows how the Preferences dialog box appears when the Java tools are installed. As you can see, the Tools item in the tree on the left side of the dialog box includes three Java tools: Compile Java, Run Java Application, and Run Java Applet. (The Run Java Applet tool is obsolete, so you can safely ignore it.)

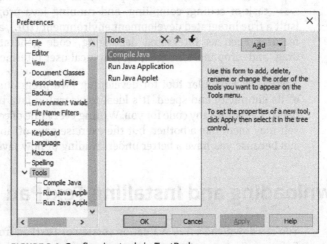

**FIGURE 2-1:** Configuring tools in TextPad.

**TIP**

If you plan on using any preview features in Java, add the `--enable-preview` and `--release 19` flags to the command line arguments for the Compile tool. The complete Compile tool arguments should look like this:

```
--enable-preview --release 19 $File
```

Then, add just the `--enable-preview` flag to the Run Java Application arguments list; the complete arguments should look like this:

```
--enable-preview $BaseName
```

**WARNING**

Do *not* add the `--release` flag to the Run Java Application tool. If you do, the tool won't be able to start the JVM, because `--release` is not a valid flag for the `java` command.

# Editing Source Files

Figure 2-2 shows a Java source file being edited in TextPad. If you've worked with a Windows text editor before, you'll have no trouble mastering the basics of TextPad. We won't go over such basic procedures as opening and saving files because they're standard; instead, we describe some TextPad features that are useful for editing Java program files.

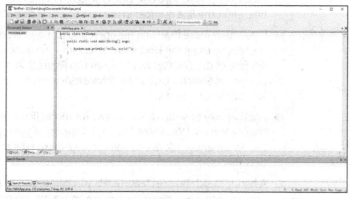

**FIGURE 2-2:** Editing a Java file in TextPad.

**TIP**

When you first create a file (by clicking the New button on the toolbar or by choosing File ⇨ New), TextPad treats the file as a normal text file, not as a Java program file. After you save the file (by clicking the Save button or choosing File ⇨ Save) and assign .java as the file extension, TextPad's Java-editing features kick in.

The following paragraphs describe some of TextPad's most note-worthy features for working with Java files:

>> You can't really tell from Figure 2-2, but TextPad uses different colors to indicate the function of each word or symbol in the program. Brackets are red so that you can spot them quickly and make sure that they're paired correctly. Keywords are blue. Comments and string literals are green. Other text, such as variable and method names, is black.

>> TextPad automatically indents whenever you type an opening bracket and then reverts to the previous indent when you type a closing bracket. This feature makes keeping your code lined up easy.

>> Line numbers display down the left edge of the editing window. You can turn these line numbers on or off by choosing View ➪ Line Numbers.

>> To go to a particular line, press Ctrl+G to bring up the Go To dialog box. Make sure that Line is selected in the Go to What box, enter the line number in the text box, and click OK.

>> If you have more than one file open, you can switch between the files by using the Document Selector — the pane on the left side of the TextPad window (refer to Figure 2-2). If the Document Selector isn't visible, choose View ➪ Document Selector to summon it.

>> Another way to switch between two (or more) files is to choose View ➪ Document Tabs. Tabs appear at the top of the document window, and you can click these tabs to switch documents.

>> A handy Match Bracket feature lets you pair brackets, braces, and parentheses. To use this feature, move the insertion point to a bracket, brace, or parenthesis and then press Ctrl+M. TextPad finds the matching element.

>> To search for text, press F5. In the Find dialog box, enter the text you're looking for, and click OK. To repeat the search, press Ctrl+F.

>> To replace text, press F8.

# Compiling a Program

To compile a Java program in TextPad, choose Tools ⇨ Compile Java or use the keyboard shortcut Ctrl+1. The javac command compiles the program, and the compiler output is displayed in the Tool Results pane of the TextPad window. If the program compiles successfully, the message Tool completed successfully appears in the Tool Results pane. If the compiler finds something wrong with your program, one or more error messages are displayed, as shown in Figure 2-3.

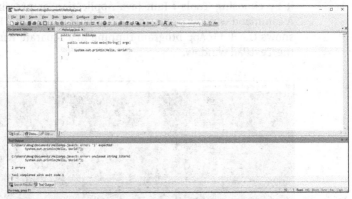

**FIGURE 2-3:** Error messages displayed by the Java compiler.

In this example, two compiler error messages are displayed:

```
C:\Users\doug\Documents\HelloApp.java:5: error: ')' expected
        System.out.println(Hello, World!");
                          ^
C:\Users\doug\Documents\HelloApp.java:5: error: unclosed string literal
        System.out.println(Hello, World!");
                                         ^
2 errors

Tool completed with exit code 1
```

TIP

If you double-click the first line of each error message, TextPad takes you to the spot where the error occurred. If you double-click the line with the unclosed string literal message, for example, you're taken to line 5, and the insertion point is positioned at the spot where the compiler found the error. Then you can correct the error and recompile the program.

**REMEMBER**

Often, a single error can cause more than one error message to display, as is the case in Figure 2-3. Here, a single mistake caused two errors.

## Running a Java Program

After you compile a Java program with no errors, you can run it by choosing Tools ➪ Run Java Application or pressing Ctrl+2. A command window opens, in which the program runs. Figure 2-4 shows the HelloApp program running in a separate window atop the TextPad window.

**FIGURE 2-4:** Running a program.

When the program finishes, the message Press any key to continue appears in the command window. When you press a key, the window closes, and TextPad comes back to life.

IN THIS CHAPTER

» Introducing the venerable Hello,
World! program

» Identifying basic elements of Java
programs such as keywords, statements,
and blocks

» Finding different ways to add comments
to your programs

» Getting basic information about object-
oriented programming

» Identifying ways to import classes

# Chapter **3**

# Java Programming Basics

I n this chapter, you find the basics of writing simple Java programs. The programs you see in this chapter are very simple:
They just display simple information on a *console* (in Windows,
that's a command-prompt window). You need to cover a few
more chapters before you start writing programs that do anything
worthwhile. But the simple programs you see in this chapter are
sufficient to illustrate the basic structure of Java programs.

Be warned that in this chapter, we introduce you to several Java
programming features that are explained in greater detail in
later chapters. You see, for example, some variable declarations,
a method, and even an if statement and a for loop. The goal of
this chapter isn't to march you into instant proficiency with these
programming elements, but just to introduce you to them.

# Looking at the Venerable Hello, World! Program

Many programming books begin with a simple example program that displays the text "Hello, World!" on the console. Listing 3-1 shows a Java program that does that.

**LISTING 3-1:** The HelloApp Program

```
public class HelloApp                              →1
{                                                  →2
    public static void main(String[] args)         →3
    {                                              →4
        System.out.println("Hello, World!");       →5
    }                                              →6
}                                                  →7
```

Later in this chapter, you discover in detail all the elements that make up this program. But first, we want to walk you through it word by word.

Lines 1 and 2 mark the declaration of a public class named HelloApp:

→1 public: A *keyword* of the Java language that indicates that the element that follows should be made available to other Java elements. In this case, what follows is a class named HelloApp. As a result, this keyword indicates that the HelloApp class is a *public class*, which means other classes can use it.

class: Another Java keyword that indicates that the element being defined here is a class. All Java programs are made up of one or more *classes*. A class definition contains code that defines the behavior of the objects created and used by the program. Although most real-world programs consist of more than one class, the simple programs you see in this chapter have just one class.

HelloApp: A *name* that identifies the class being defined here. Whereas keywords, such as public and class, are words that are defined by the Java programming language, names are words that you create to identify various elements you use in your program. In this case, the name HelloApp identifies the public class being defined here. (Although *name* is the technically correct term, sometimes names are called *identifiers*. Technically, a name is a type of identifier, but not all identifiers are names.)

→2   {: The opening brace on line 2 marks the beginning of the *body* of the class. The end of the body is marked by the closing brace on line 7. Everything that appears within these braces belongs to the class. As you work with Java, you'll find that it uses these braces a lot. Pretty soon the third and fourth fingers on your right hand will know exactly where they are on the keyboard.

Lines 3 through 7 define a *method* of the HelloApp class named main:

→3   public: The public keyword is used again, this time to indicate that a method being declared here should have public access. That means classes other than the HelloApp class can use it. All Java programs must have a class that declares a public method named main. The main method contains the statements that are executed when you run the program.

static: The Java language requires that you specify static when you declare the main method.

void: In Java, a *method* is a unit of code that can calculate and return a value. For example, you could create a method that calculates a sales total. Then the sales total would be the return value of the method. If a method doesn't need to return a value, you must use the void keyword to indicate that no value is returned. Because Java requires that the main method not return a value, you must specify void when you declare the main method.

main: Finally, here's the *identifier* that provides the name for this method. As we've already mentioned, Java requires that this method be named main. Besides the main method, you can create additional methods with whatever names you want to use. You discover how to create additional methods in Chapter 8. Until then, the programs consist of just one method named main.

(`String[] args`): Oh, boy. This Java element is too advanced to thoroughly explain just yet. It's called a *parameter list,* and it's used to pass data to a method. Java requires that the `main` method must receive a single parameter that's an array of `String` objects. By convention, this parameter is named `args`. If you don't know what a parameter, a `String`, or an array is, don't worry about it. You can find out what a `String` is in the next chapter, and parameters are in Chapter 8; arrays are in Chapter 12. In the meantime, realize that you have to code (`String[] args`) on the declaration for the `main` methods in all your programs.

→4   Another {: Another set of braces begins at line 4 and ends at line 6. These braces mark the body of the `main` method. Notice that the closing brace in line 6 is paired with the opening brace in line 4, whereas the closing brace in line 7 is paired with the one in line 2. This type of pairing is commonplace in Java. In short, whenever you come to a closing brace, it's paired with the most recent opening brace that hasn't already been closed — that is, that hasn't already been paired with a closing brace.

→5   `System.out.println("Hello, World!");`: This is the only statement in the entire program. It calls a method named `println` that belongs to the `System.out` object. The `println` method displays a line of text on the console. The text to be displayed is passed to the `println` method as a parameter in parentheses following the word `println`. In this case, the text is the string literal `Hello, World!` enclosed in a set of quotation marks. As a result, this statement displays the text `Hello, World!` on the console.

Note that in Java, most (but not all) statements must end with a semicolon. Because this statement is the only one in the program, this line is the only one that requires a semicolon.

→6   }: Line 6 contains the closing brace that marks the end of the `main` method body that was begun by the brace on line 4.

→7   Another }: Line 7 contains the closing brace that marks the end of the `HelloApp` class body that was begun by the brace on line 2. Because this program consists of just one class, this line also marks the end of the program.

To run this program, you must first use a text editor such as Notepad or TextPad to enter it — exactly as it appears in Listing 3-1 — in a text file named `HelloApp.java`. Then you can compile it by running the following command at a command prompt (refer to Chapter 13):

```
javac HelloApp.java
```

This command creates a class file named HelloApp.class that contains the Java bytecode compiled for the HelloApp class.

You can run the program by entering this command (again, check out Chapter 13):

```
java HelloApp
```

Now that you've seen what a Java program actually looks like, you're in a better position to understand exactly what this command does. First, it loads the Java Virtual Machine (JVM) into memory. Then it locates the HelloApp class, which must be contained in a file named HelloApp.class. Finally, it runs the main method of the HelloApp class. The main method, in turn, displays the message "Hello, World!" on the console.

**TIP**

Because the HelloApp.java file contains just one class, you can run it directly using the java command without first compiling. If you type **java HelloApp** and there is a .java file but no corresponding .class file, the java command will first compile the HelloApp.java file and then run the resulting class.

The rest of this chapter describes some of the basic elements of the Java programming language in greater detail.

# Dealing with Keywords

A *keyword* is a word that has a special meaning defined by the Java programming language. The program shown earlier in Listing 3-1 uses four keywords: public, class, static, and void. In all, Java has 53 keywords. They're listed in alphabetical order in Table 3-1.

**WARNING**

Like everything else in Java, keywords are case-sensitive. Thus, if you type If instead of if or For instead of for, the compiler complains about your error. Because Visual Basic keywords begin with capital letters, you'll make this mistake frequently if you've programmed in Visual Basic.

**TABLE 3-1** Java's Keywords

| | | | |
|---|---|---|---|
| abstract | false | open | throws |
| assert | final | opens | to |
| boolean | finally | permits | transient |
| break | float | protected | transitive |
| byte | for | provides | true |
| case | if | public | try |
| catch | implements | record | uses |
| char | import | requires | var |
| class | instanceof | return | void |
| const | int | sealed | volatile |
| continue | interface | short | while |
| do | long | static | with |
| double | module | strictfp | yield |
| else | native | super | _ (underscore) |
| enum | new | switch | |
| exports | non-sealed | synchronized | |
| extends | null | throw | |

Considering the Java community's disdain for Visual Basic, it's surprising that the error messages generated when you capitalize keywords aren't more insulting. Accidentally capitalizing a keyword in Visual Basic style can really throw the Java compiler for a loop. Consider this program, which contains the single error of capitalizing the word For:

```
public class CaseApp
{
    public static void main(String[] args)
    {
        For (int i = 0; i<5; i++)
```

```
        System.out.println("Hi");
    }
}
```

When you try to compile this program, the compiler generates a total of four error messages for this one mistake:

```
C:\Users\doug\Documents\CaseApp.java:5: error: '.class' expected
        For (int i = 0; i<5; i++)
            ^
C:\Users\doug\Documents\CaseApp.java:5: error: illegal start of type
        For (int i = 0; i<5; i++)
                 ^
C:\Users\doug\Documents\CaseApp.java:5: error: not a statement
        For (int i = 0; i<5; i++)
             ^
C:\Users\doug\Documents\CaseApp.java:5: error: ';' expected
        For (int i = 0; i<5; i++)
                        ^

4 errors
```

Even though this single mistake generates four error messages, not one of the messages actually points to the problem. The little arrow beneath the source line indicates what part of the line is in error, and none of these error messages has the arrow pointing anywhere near the word For! The compiler isn't smart enough to realize that you meant for instead of For. So it treats For as a legitimate identifier and then complains about everything else on the line that follows it. It would be much more helpful if the compiler generated an error message like this:

```
C:\Java Essentials\CaseApp.java:5: 'For' is not a keyword
For (int i = 0; i<5; i++)
```

Better yet, for those of us old enough to remember *Get Smart* on TV:

```
C:\Java Essentials\CaseApp.java:5: Theese ees Java! Vee do not
    capitalize keyverds here!
For (int i = 0; i<5; i++)
```

**REMEMBER**

The moral of the story is that Java is case-sensitive, and if your program won't compile and the error messages don't make any sense, check for keywords that you've mistakenly capitalized.

# Working with Statements

Like most programming languages, Java uses statements to build programs. Unlike most programming languages, Java doesn't use statements as its fundamental unit of code. Instead, it gives that honor to the class. However, every class must have a body, and the body of a class is made up of one or more statements. In other words, you can't have a meaningful Java program without at least one statement. The following sections describe the ins and outs of working with Java statements.

## Types of statements

Java has many types of statements. Some statements simply create variables that you can use to store data. These types of statements are often called *declaration statements* and tend to look like this:

```
int i;
String name;
```

Another common type of statement is an *assignment statement*, which assigns a value to a variable:

```
i = 42;
name = "Jackie Robinson";
```

Declaration and assignment statements can be combined into a single statement, like this:

```
int i = 42;
String name = "Jackie Robinson";
```

Another common type of statement is an *expression statement*, which performs calculations or other operations. For example:

```
System.out.println("Hello, World!");
```

Notice that this statement is the same as line 5 in Listing 3-1. Thus the single statement in the HelloApp program is an expression statement.

There are many kinds of statements besides these two. if statements, for example, execute other statements only if a particular condition has been met, and statements such as `for,` `while,` and `do` execute whole groups of statements repeatedly.

It's often said that every Java statement must end with a semicolon. Actually, this isn't quite true. *Some* types of Java statements must end with semicolons — but others don't have to. The basic rule is that declaration and expression statements must end with a semicolon, but most other statement types do not. Where this rule gets tricky, however, is that most other types of statements include one or more declarations or expression statements that do use semicolons. Here's a typical `if` statement:

```
if (total > 100)
    discountPercent = 10;
```

Here, the variable named `discountPercent` is given a value of `10` if the value of the `total` variable is greater than `100`. The assignment statement ends with a semicolon, but the `if` statement itself doesn't. (The Java compiler lets you know if you use a semicolon when you shouldn't.)

## White space

In Java, the term *white space* refers to one or more consecutive space characters, tab characters, or line breaks. All white space is considered the same.

In other words, a single space is treated the same as a tab or line break or any combination of spaces, tabs, and line breaks.

If you've programmed in Visual Basic, white space is different from what you're used to. In Visual Basic, line breaks mark the end of statements unless special continuation characters are used. In Java, you don't have to do anything special to continue a statement onto a second line. Thus the statement

```
x = (y + 5) / z;
```

is identical to this statement:

```
x =
(y + 5) / z;
```

Be advised, however, that you can't put white space in the middle of a keyword or identifier. The following example won't work:

```
p u b l i c static v o i d main(String[] args)
```

Here the extra spaces between the letters in the words *public* and *void* will confuse the compiler.

TIP

Using white space liberally in your programs is a good idea. In particular, you should routinely use white space like this:

>> **Line breaks:** Place each statement on a separate line. In addition, you can break a longer statement into several lines for clarity.

>> **Tabs or spaces:** Use tabs or spaces to line up elements that belong together.

The compiler ignores the extra white space, so it doesn't affect the bytecode that's created for your program. As a result, using extra white space in your program doesn't affect your program's performance in any way, but it does make the program's source code easier to read.

# Working with Blocks

A *block* is a group of one or more statements that's enclosed in braces. A block begins with an opening brace ({) and ends with a closing brace (}). Between the opening and closing braces, you can code one or more statements. Here's a block that consists of three statements:

```
{
    int i, j;
    i = 100;
    j = 200;
}
```

TIP

You can code the braces that mark a block in two popular ways. One is to place both braces on separate lines and then indent the statements that make up the block. For example:

```
if ( i > 0)
{
    String s = "The value of i is " + i;
    System.out.print(s);
}
```

The other style is to place the opening brace for the block on the same line as the statement the block is associated with, like this:

```
if ( i > 0) {
    String s = "The value of i is " + i;
    System.out.print(s);
}
```

Which style you use is a matter of personal preference. We prefer the first style, and that's the style we use throughout this book. But either style works — and many programmers prefer the second style because it's more concise.

Note that even though a block can be treated as a single statement, you should *not* end a block with a semicolon. The statements within the block may require semicolons, but the block itself does not.

**TIP**

# Creating Identifiers

An *identifier* is a word that you make up to refer to a Java programming element by name. Although you can assign identifiers to many types of Java elements, they're most commonly used for the following elements:

>> Classes, such as the HelloApp class in Listing 3-1

>> Methods, such as the main method in Listing 3-1

>> Variables and fields, which hold data used by your program

>> Parameters, which pass data values to methods

You must follow a few simple rules when you create identifiers:

**REMEMBER**

>> Identifiers are case-sensitive. As a result, SalesTax and salesTax are distinct identifiers.

>> Identifiers can be made up of upper- or lowercase letters, numerals, underscore characters (_), and dollar signs ($). Thus, identifier names such as Port1, SalesTax$, and Total_Sales.

>> All identifiers must begin with a letter. Thus, a15 is a valid identifier, but 13Unlucky isn't (because it begins with a numeral).

>> An identifier can't be the same as any of the Java keywords listed in bold type in Table 3-1. Thus, you can't create a variable named for or a class named public. (To avoid confusion, we recommend you avoid the contextual keywords — the ones that aren't in bold type in Table 3-1 — as well.)

>> The Java language specification recommends that you avoid using dollar signs in names you create, because code generators use dollar signs to create identifiers. Thus, avoiding dollar signs helps you avoid creating names that conflict with generated names.

# Crafting Comments

A *comment* is a bit of text that provides explanations of your code. The compiler ignores comments, so you can place any text you want in a comment. Using plenty of comments in your program is a good way to explain what your program does and how it works.

Java has two basic types of comments: *end-of-line comments* and *traditional comments.* More about that is coming right up.

## End-of-line comments

An *end-of-line comment* begins with the sequence // (a pair of consecutive slashes) and ends at the end of the line. You can place an end-of-line comment at the end of any line. Everything you type after the // is ignored by the compiler. For example:

```
total = total * discountPercent; // calculate the discounted total
```

If you want, you can also place end-of-line comments on separate lines, like this:

```
// calculate the discounted total
total = total * discountPercent;
```

You can place end-of-line comments in the middle of statements that span two or more lines. For example:

```
total = (total * discountPercent) // apply the discount first
    + salesTax; // then add the sales tax
```

## Traditional comments

A *traditional comment* begins with the sequence /*, ends with the sequence */, and can span multiple lines. Here's an example:

```
/* HelloApp sample program.
This program demonstrates the basic structure
that all Java programs must follow. */
```

A traditional comment can begin and end anywhere on a line. If you want, you can even sandwich a comment between other Java programming elements, like this:

```
x = (y + /* a strange place for a comment */ 5) / z;
```

Usually, traditional comments appear on separate lines. One common use for traditional comments is to place a block of comment lines at the beginning of a class to indicate information about the class — such as what the class does, who wrote it, and so on. That type of comment, however, is usually better coded as a JavaDoc comment, as described in the next section.

# Introducing Object-Oriented Programming

Having presented some of the most basic elements of the Java programming language, most Java books would next turn to the important topics of variables and data types. Because Java is an inherently object-oriented programming language, however, and because classes are the heart of object-oriented programming, we look next at classes to explore the important role they play in creating objects. We get to variables and data types first thing in the next chapter.

# Understanding classes and objects

As we've already mentioned, a *class* is code that defines the behavior of a Java programming element called an object. An *object* is an entity that has both state and behavior. The *state* of an object consists of any data that the object might be keeping track of, and the *behavior* consists of *actions* that the object can perform. The behaviors are represented in the class by one or more methods that can be called on to perform actions.

The difference between a class and an object is similar to the difference between a blueprint and a house. A blueprint is a plan for a house. A house is an implementation of a blueprint. One set of blueprints can be used to build many houses. Likewise, a class is a plan for an object, and an object is — in Java terms — an *instance* of a class. You can use a single class to create more than one object.

When an object is created, Java sets aside an area of computer memory that's sufficient to hold all the data that's stored by the object. As a result, each instance of a class has its own data, independent of the data used by other instances of the same class.

# Understanding static methods

You don't necessarily have to create an instance of a class to use the methods of the class. If you declare a method with the static keyword, you can call the method without first creating an instance of the class, because static methods are called from classes, not from objects.

The main method of a Java application must be declared with the static keyword because when you start a Java program by using the java command from a command prompt, Java doesn't create an instance of the application class. Instead, it simply calls the program's static main method.

The difference between static and nonstatic methods will become more apparent when you look at object-oriented programming in more depth in Chapters 10 and 11. But for now, consider this analogy. The blueprints for a house include the details about systems that actually perform work in a finished house, such as electrical and plumbing systems. To use those systems, you have to actually build a house. In other words, you can't turn on the hot water by using the blueprint alone; you have to have an actual house with an actual device to heat the water.

The blueprints do include detailed measurements of the dimensions of the house, however. As a result, you *can* use the blueprints to determine the square footage of the living room.

Now imagine that the blueprints actually have a built-in calculator that displays the size of the living room if you push the Living Room button. That button would be like a static method in a class: You don't actually have to build a house to use the button; you can activate it from the blueprints alone.

Many Java programs are entirely made up of static methods. Most realistic programs, however, require that you create one or more objects that the program uses as it executes. As a result, knowing how to create simple classes and how to create objects from those classes are basic skills in Java programming.

## Creating an object from a class

In Java, you can create an object from a class in several ways. The most straightforward way is to create a variable that provides a name you can use to refer to the object, use the new keyword to create an instance of the class, and then assign the resulting object to the variable. The general form of a statement that does that bit of magic looks like this:

```
ClassName variableName = new ClassName();
```

To create an object instance of a class named Class1 and assign it to a variable named myClass1Object, you would write a statement like this:

```
Class1 myClass1Object = new Class1();
```

Why do you have to list the class name twice? The first time, you're providing a *type* for the variable. In other words, you're saying that the variable you're creating here can be used to hold objects created from the Class1 class. The second time you list the class name, you're creating an object from the class. The new keyword tells Java to create an object, and the class name provides the name of the class to use to create the object.

You may have noticed that in the variable name myClass1Object, we capitalized the words Class1 and Object within the name, but did not capitalize the first letter of the name. This type of capitalization is called *camel case*, because the capitalized parts of the word look like the humps on a camel's back. Camel case is commonly used for variable names in Java.

The equal sign (=) is an *assignment operator*. It simply says to take the object created by the new keyword and assign it to the variable. Thus, this statement actually does *three* things:

>> It creates a variable named myClass1Object that can be used to hold objects created from the Class1 class. At this point, no object has been created — just a variable that can be used to store objects.

>> It creates a new object in memory from the Class1 class.

>> It assigns this newly created object to the myClass1Object variable. That way, you can use the myClassObject variable to refer to the object that was created.

## Viewing a program that uses an object

To give you an early look at what object-oriented programming really looks like, Listing 3-2 and Listing 3-3 show another version of the HelloApp application — this time using two classes, one of which is actually made into an object when the program is run. The first class, named HelloApp2, is shown in Listing 3-2. This class is similar to the HelloApp class shown in Listing 3-1 but uses an object created from the second class, named Greeter, to actually display the "Hello, World!" message on the console. The Greeter class is shown in Listing 3-3. It defines a method named sayHello that displays the message.

Both the HelloApp and the Greeter classes are public classes. Java requires that each public class be stored in a separate file with the same name as the class; the filename ends with the extension .java. As a result, the HelloApp2 class is stored in a file named HelloApp2.java, and the Greeter class is stored in a file named Greeter.java.

### The HelloApp2 class

The HelloApp2 class is shown in Listing 3-2.

LISTING 3-2: **The HelloApp2 Class**

```
// This application displays a hello message on      →1
// the console by creating an instance of the
// Greeter class and then calling the Greeter
// object's sayHello method.
public class HelloApp2                               →5
{
public static void main(String[] args)              →7
    {
        Greeter myGreeterObject = new Greeter();     →9
        myGreeterObject.sayHello();                 →10
    }
}
```

The following paragraphs describe the key points:

→1   This class begins with a series of comment lines identifying the function of the program. For these comments, we used simple end-of-line comments rather than traditional comments. (For more on commenting, see the "Crafting Comments" section, earlier in this chapter.)

→5   The HelloApp2 class begins on line 5 with the public class declaration. Because the public keyword is used, a file named HelloApp2.java must contain this class.

→7   The main method is declared, using the same signature as the main method in the first version of this program (Listing 3-1). Get used to this form, because *all* Java applications must include a main method that's declared in this way.

→9   The first line in the body of the main method creates a variable named myGreeterObject that can hold objects created from the Greeter class. Then it creates a new object using the Greeter class and assigns this object to the myGreeterObject variable.

→10   The second line in the body of the main method calls the myGreeterObject object's sayHello method. As you'll see in a moment, this method simply displays the message "Hello, World!" on the console.

## The Greeter class

The Greeter class is shown in Listing 3-3.

---

**LISTING 3-3:** **The Greeter Class**

```
// This class represents a Greeter object that
displays                                            →1
// a hello message on the console.
public class Greeter                                →3
{
public void sayHello()                              →5
    {
        System.out.println("Hello, World!");        →7
    }
}
```

---

The following paragraphs describe the key points:

→1  This class also begins with a series of comment lines that
    identify the function of the program.

→3  The class declaration begins on this line. The class is
    declared as public so other classes can use it. Strictly
    speaking, the public declaration here isn't strictly required;
    the HelloApp2 class can access the Greeter class without
    it because they're in the same package.

→5  The sayHello method is declared using the public
    keyword so that it's available to other classes that use the
    Greeter class. The void keyword indicates that this method
    doesn't provide any data back to the statement that calls it,
    and sayHello simply provides the name of the method.

→7  The body of this method consists of just one line of code
    that displays the "Hello, World!" message on
    the console.

## So what's the difference?

You may notice that the only line that actually does any real
work in the HelloApp2 program is line 7 in the Greeter class
(Listing 3-3), and this line happens to be identical to line 5 in
the original HelloApp class (Listing 3-1). Other than the fact

that the second version requires roughly twice as much code as the first version, what really *is* the difference between these two applications?

Simply put, the first version is procedural, and the second is object-oriented. In the first version of the program, the `main` method of the application class does all the work of the application by itself: It just says hello. The second version defines a class that knows how to say hello to the world and then creates an object from that class and asks that object to say hello. The application itself doesn't know (or even care) exactly how the `Greeter` object says hello. It doesn't know exactly what the greeting will be, what language the greeting will be in, or even how the greeting will be displayed.

To illustrate this point, consider what would happen if you used the `Greeter` class shown in Listing 3-4 rather than the one shown in Listing 3-3. This version of the `Greeter` class uses a Java library class called `JOptionPane` to display a message in a dialog box rather than in a console window. (We won't bother explaining in a list how this code works, but you can find out more about it in the next chapter.) If you were to run the `HelloApp2` application using this version of the `Greeter` class, you'd get the dialog box shown in Figure 3-1.

**LISTING 3-4:** **Another Version of the Greeter Class**

```
// This class creates a Greeter object that displays
// a hello message in a dialog box.

import javax.swing.JOptionPane;                          →4

public class Greeter
{
    public void sayHello()
    {
        JOptionPane.showMessageDialog(null,
            "Hello, World!", "Greeter",
            JOptionPane.INFORMATION_MESSAGE);
    }
}
```

**FIGURE 3-1:** The class in Listing 3-4 displays this dialog box.

REMEMBER

The important point to realize here is that the HelloApp2 class doesn't have to be changed to use this new version of the Greeter class. Instead, all you have to do is replace the old Greeter class with the new one, recompile the Greeter class, and the HelloApp2 class won't know the difference. That's one of the main benefits of object-oriented programming.

# Importing Java API Classes

You may have noticed that the Greeter class in Listing 3-4 includes this statement:

```
import javax.swing.JOptionPane;
```

The purpose of the import statement is to let the compiler know that the program is using a class that's defined by the Java API called JOptionPane.

Because the Java API contains literally thousands of classes, some form of organization is needed to make the classes easier to access. Java does this by grouping classes into manageable groups called *packages*. In the previous example, the package that contains the JOptionPane class is named javax.swing.

Strictly speaking, import statements are never required. But if you don't use import statements to import the API classes your program uses, you must *fully qualify* the names of the classes when you use them by listing the package name in front of the class name. So if the class in Listing 3-4 didn't include the import statement in line 4, you'd have to code line 11 like this:

```
javax.swing.JOptionPane.showMessageDialog(null,
    "Hello, World!", "Greeter",
    javax.swing.JOptionPane.INFORMATION_MESSAGE);
```

In other words, you'd have to specify javax.swing.JOptionPane instead of just JOptionPane whenever you referred to this class.

TIP

Here are some additional rules for working with import statements:

>> import statements must appear at the beginning of the class file, before any class declarations.

>> You can include as many import statements as are necessary to import all the classes used by your program.

>> You can import all the classes in a particular package by listing the package name followed by an asterisk wildcard, like this:

```
import javax.swing.*;
```

>> Because many programs use the classes that are contained in the java.lang package, you don't have to import that package. Instead, those classes are automatically available to all programs. The System class is defined in the java.lang package. As a result, you don't have to provide an import statement to use this class.

# Chapter 4

# Working with Variables and Data Types

I n this chapter, you find out the basics of working with variables in Java. Variables are the key to making Java programs general purpose. Variables are also the key to creating programs that can perform calculations. Suppose that you want to create a program that calculates the area of a circle, given the circle's radius. Such a program uses two variables: one to represent the radius of the circle and the other to represent the circle's area. The program asks the user to enter a value for the first variable. Then it calculates the value of the second variable.

## Declaring Variables

In Java, you must explicitly declare all variables before using them. This rule is in contrast to some languages — most notably Python, which lets you use variables that haven't been explicitly declared.

WARNING

Allowing you to use variables that you haven't explicitly declared might seem a pretty good idea at first glance, but it's a common source of bugs that result from misspelled variable names. Java requires that you explicitly declare variables so that if you misspell a variable name, the compiler can detect your mistake and display a compiler error.

The basic form of a variable declaration is this:

```
type name;
```

Here are some examples:

```
int x;
String lastName;
double radius;
```

In these examples, variables named x, lastName, and radius are declared. The x variable holds integer values, the lastName variable holds String values, and the radius variable holds double values. For more information about what these types mean, see the section "Working with Primitive Data Types" later in this chapter. Until then, just realize that int variables can hold whole numbers (such as 5, 1,340, or -34), double variables can hold numbers with fractional parts (such as 0.5, 99.97, or 3.1415), and String variables can hold text values (such as "Hello, World!" or "Jason P. Finch").

**TIP**

Notice that variable declarations end with semicolons. That's because a variable declaration is itself a type of statement.

**REMEMBER**

Variable names follow the same rules as other Java identifiers, as we describe in Chapter 3, so see that chapter for details. In short, a variable name can be any combination of letters, numerals, or underscores and dollar signs but must start with a letter, an underscore (_), or a dollar sign ($). Most programmers prefer to start variable names with lowercase letters and capitalize the first letter of individual words within the name. firstName and salesTaxRate, for example, are typical variable names. (As we mention in the preceding chapter, this is called *camel case* because the capital letters in the middle of the names look like humps on the back of a camel.)

# Declaring two or more variables in one statement

You can declare two or more variables of the same type in a single statement by separating the variable names with commas. For example:

```
int x, y, z;
```

Here three variables of type int are declared, using the names x, y, and z.

**TIP**

As a rule, we suggest that you avoid declaring multiple variables in a single statement. Your code is easier to read and maintain if you give each variable a separate declaration.

# Declaring class variables

A *class variable* is a variable that any method in a class can access, including static methods such as main. When declaring a class variable, you have two basic rules to follow:

>> You must place the declaration within the body of the class but not within any of the class methods.

>> You must include the word static in the declaration. The word static comes before the variable type.

**TIP**

Class variables are often called *static variables.* The key distinction between a static variable and an instance variable, which we cover in the next section, is that the value of a static variable is the same for all instances of the class. In contrast, each instance of a class has distinct values for its instance variables.

The following program shows the proper way to declare a class variable named helloMessage:

```
public class HelloApp
{
    static String helloMessage;

    public static void main(String[] args)
    {
        helloMessage = "Hello, World!";
        System.out.println(helloMessage);
```

```
        }
    }
```

As you can see, the declaration includes the word static and is placed within the HelloApp class body but not within the body of the main method.

TIP

You don't have to place class variable declarations at the beginning of a class. Some programmers prefer to place them at the end of the class, as in this example:

```
public class HelloApp
{
    public static void main(String[] args)
    {
        helloMessage = "Hello, World!";
        System.out.println(helloMessage);
    }

    static String helloMessage;
}
```

Here the helloMessage variable is declared *after* the main method.

TIP

We think classes are easier to read if the variables are declared first, so that's where you see them in this book.

## Declaring instance variables

An *instance variable* is similar to a class variable but doesn't specify the word static in its declaration. As the name suggests, instance variables are associated with instances of classes. As a result, you can use them only when you create an instance of a class. Because static methods aren't associated with an instance of the class, you can't use an instance variable in a static method — and that includes the main method.

The following example program won't compile:

```
public class HelloApp
{
    String helloMessage;

    public static void main(String[] args)
    {
```

```
        helloMessage = "Hello, World!";
        System.out.println(helloMessage); // will not compile
    }
}
```

If you try to compile this program, you get the following error messages:

```
C:\Java\HelloApp.java:7: error: non-static variable helloMessage cannot
    be referenced from a static context
helloMessage = "Hello, World!";
^
C:\Java\HelloApp.java:8: non-static variable helloMessage cannot be
    referenced from a static context
System.out.println(helloMessage);
                ^
```

Both of these errors occur because the main method is static, so it can't access instance variables.

Instance variables are useful whenever you create your own classes, but because we don't cover that topic until Chapter 10, you won't see many examples of instance methods until then.

## Declaring local variables

A *local variable* is a variable that's declared within the body of a method. Then you can use the variable only within that method. Other methods in the class aren't even aware that the variable exists.

Here's a version of the HelloApp class in which the helloMessage variable is declared as a local variable:

```
public class HelloApp
{
    public static void main(String[] args)
    {
        String helloMessage;
        helloMessage = "Hello, World!";
        System.out.println(helloMessage);
    }
}
```

Note that you don't specify static on a declaration for a local variable. If you do, the compiler generates an error message and refuses to compile your program. Local variables always exist within the scope of a method, and they exist only while that method is executing. As a result, whether an instance of the class has been created is irrelevant. (For more information, see the section "Understanding Scope," later in this chapter.)

TIP

Unlike class and instance variables, a local variable is fussy about where you position the declaration for it. In particular, you must place the declaration before the first statement that actually uses the variable. Thus the following program won't compile:

```
public class HelloApp
{
    public static void main(String[] args)
    {
        helloMessage = "Hello, World!"; // error -- helloMessage
        System.out.println(helloMessage); // is not yet declared
        String helloMessage;
    }
}
```

When it gets to the first line of the main method, the compiler generates two error messages complaining that it can't find the symbol "helloMessage". That's because the symbol hasn't been declared.

Although most local variables are declared near the beginning of a method's body, you can also declare local variables within smaller blocks of code marked by braces. This will make more sense to you when you read about statements that use blocks, such as if and for statements. But here's an example:

```
if (taxRate > 0)
{
    double taxAmount;
    taxAmount = subTotal * taxRate;
    total = subTotal + total;
}
```

Here the variable taxAmount exists only within the set of braces that belongs to the if statement. (You can assume that the variables taxRate, subtotal, and total are defined outside of the code block defined by the braces.)

# Initializing Variables

In Java, local variables are not given initial default values. The compiler checks to make sure that you have assigned a value before you use a local variable. The following example program won't compile:

```
public class TestApp
{
    public static void main(String[] args)
    {
        int i;
        System.out.println("The value of i is " + i);
    }
}
```

If you try to compile this program, you get the following error message:

```
C:\Java\TestApp.java:6: error: variable i might not have been
    initialized
System.out.println("The value of i is " + i);
                                          ^
```

To avoid this error message, you must initialize local variables before you use them. You can do that by using an assignment statement or an initializer, as we describe in the following sections.

**TIP**

Unlike local variables, class variables and instance variables are given default values. Numeric types are automatically initialized to zero, and String variables are initialized to empty strings. As a result, you don't have to initialize a class variable or an instance variable, although you can if you want them to have an initial value other than the default.

# Initializing variables with assignment statements

One way to initialize a variable is to code an *assignment statement* following the variable declaration. Assignment statements have this general form:

```
variable = expression;
```

Here, the `expression` can be any Java expression that yields a value of the same type as the variable. Here's a version of the `main` method from the previous example that correctly initializes the `i` variable before using it:

```java
public static void main(String[] args)
{
    int i;
    i = 0;
    System.out.println("i is " + i);
}
```

In this example, the variable is initialized to a value of zero before the `println` method is called to print the variable's value.

You find out a lot more about expressions in Chapter 5. For now, you can just use simple literal values, such as 0 in this example.

## Initializing variables with initializers

Java also allows you to initialize a variable on the same statement that declares the variable. To do that, you use an *initializer*, which has the following general form:

```
type name = expression;
```

In effect, the initializer lets you combine a declaration and an assignment statement into one concise statement. Here are some examples:

```java
int x = 0;
String lastName = "Lowe";
double radius = 15.4;
```

In each case, the variable is both declared and initialized in a single statement.

When you declare more than one variable in a single statement, each variable can have its own initializer. The following code declares variables named x and y, and initializes x to 5 and y to 10:

```
int x = 5, y = 10;
```

When you declare two class or instance variables in a single statement but use only one initializer, you can mistakenly think that the initializer applies to both variables. Consider this statement:

```
static int x, y = 5;
```

Here you might think that both x and y would initialize to 5. But the initializer applies only to y, so x is initialized to its default value, 0. (If you make this mistake with a local variable, the compiler displays an error message for the first statement that uses the x variable because it isn't properly initialized.)

# Using Final Variables (Constants)

A *final variable* is a variable whose value you can't change after it's been initialized. To declare a final variable, you add the final keyword to the variable declaration, like this:

```
final int WEEKDAYS = 5;
```

A variable that is both final and static is called a *constant.* Constants are often used for values that are universally the same, such as the number of days in June or the atomic weight of iridium. To create a constant, add static final to the declaration, as follows:

```
static final int WEEKDAYS = 5;
```

Although it isn't required, using all capital letters for final variable names is common. When you do so, you can easily spot the use of constants in your programs.

In addition to values that are universally the same, constants are useful for values that are used in several places throughout a program and that don't change during the course of the program. Suppose that you're writing a game that features bouncing balls, and you want the balls always to have a radius of 6 pixels. This program probably needs to use the ball diameter in several places — to draw the ball onscreen, to determine whether the ball has hit a wall, to determine whether the ball has hit another ball, and so on. Rather than just specify 6 whenever you need the ball's radius, you can set up a class constant named BALL_RADIUS, like this:

```
static final int BALL_RADIUS = 6;
```

Using a constant has two advantages:

>> If you decide later that the radius of the balls should be 7, you make the change in just one place: the initializer for the BALL_RADIUS constant.

>> The constant helps document the inner workings of your program. The operation of a complicated calculation that uses the ball's radius is easier to understand if it specifies BALL_RADIUS rather than 6, for example.

# Working with Primitive Data Types

The term *data type* refers to the type of data that can be stored in a variable. Java is sometimes called a *strongly typed* language because when you declare a variable, you must specify the variable's type. Then the compiler ensures that you don't try to assign data of the wrong type to the variable. The following example code generates a compiler error:

```
int x;
x = 3.1415;
```

Because x is declared as a variable of type int (which holds whole numbers), you can't assign the value 3.1415 to it.

REMEMBER

Java makes an important distinction between primitive types and reference types.

>> **Primitive types** are the data types defined by the language itself.

>> **Reference types** are types defined by classes in the Java application programming interface (API) or by classes you create rather than by the language itself.

A key difference between a primitive type and a reference type is that the memory location associated with a primitive-type variable contains the actual value of the variable. As a result, primitive types are sometimes called *value types*. By contrast, the memory location associated with a reference-type variable contains an address (called a *pointer*) that indicates the memory location of the actual object. We explain reference types more fully in the section "Using reference types," later in this chapter, so don't worry if this explanation doesn't make sense just yet.

Java defines a total of eight primitive types, listed in Table 4-1. Of the eight primitive types, six are for numbers, one is for characters, and one is for true/false values.

**TABLE 4-1** Java's Primitive Types

| Type | Explanation |
|------|-------------|
| int | A 32-bit (4-byte) integer value |
| byte | An 8-bit (1-byte) integer value |
| short | A 16-bit (2-byte) integer value |
| long | A 64-bit (8-byte) integer value |
| float | A 32-bit (4-byte) floating-point value |
| double | A 64-bit (8-byte) floating-point value |
| char | A 16-bit character using the Unicode encoding scheme |
| boolean | A true or false value |

## Integer types

An *integer* is a whole number — that is, a number with no fractional or decimal portion. Java has four integer types, which you can use to store numbers of varying sizes. The most commonly used integer type is `int`. This type uses 4 bytes to store an integer value that can range from about negative 2 billion to positive 2 billion.

If you're writing the application that counts how many hamburgers McDonald's has sold, an `int` variable may not be big enough. In that case, you can use a `long` integer instead. `long` is a 64-bit integer that can hold numbers ranging from about negative 9,000 trillion to positive 9,000 trillion. (That's a big number, even by federal deficit standards.)

In some cases, you may not need integers as large as the standard `int` type provides. For those cases, Java provides two smaller integer types. The `short` type represents a two-byte integer, which can hold numbers from −32,768 to +32,767, and the `byte` type defines a single-byte integer that can range from −128 to +127.

Although the `short` and `byte` types require less memory than the `int` and `long` types, there's usually little reason to use them for desktop applications, where memory is usually plentiful. A few bytes here or there won't make any difference in the performance of most programs — so you should stick to `int` and `long` most of the time. Also, use `long` only when you know that you're dealing with numbers too large for `int`.

**TIP**

Java allows you to *promote* an integer type to a larger integer type. Java allows the following, for example:

```
int xInt;
long yLong;
xInt = 32;
yLong = xInt;
```

Here you can assign the value of the xInt variable to the yLong variable because yLong is larger than xInt. Java does not allow the converse, however:

```
int xInt;
long yLong;
yLong = 32;
xInt = yLong;
```

The value of the yLong variable cannot be assigned to the xInt because xInt is smaller than yLong. Because this assignment may result in a loss of data, Java doesn't allow it.

You can include underscores to make longer numbers easier to read. Thus, the following statements both assign the same value to the variables xLong1 and xLong2:

```
long xLong1 = 58473882;
long xLong2 = 58_473_882;
```

## Floating-point types

*Floating-point* numbers are numbers that have fractional parts (usually expressed with a decimal point), such as 19.95 or 3.1415.

Java has two primitive types for floating-point numbers: float, which uses 4 bytes, and double, which uses 8 bytes. In almost all cases, you should use the double type whenever you need numbers with fractional values.

The *precision* of a floating-point value indicates how many significant digits the value can have following its decimal point. The precision of a float type is only about six or seven decimal digits, which isn't sufficient for many types of calculations.

By contrast, double variables have a precision of about 15 digits, which is enough for most purposes.

When you use a floating-point literal, we suggest you always include a decimal point, like this:

```
double period = 99.0;
```

That avoids the confusion of assigning what looks like an integer to a floating-point variable.

If you do use a decimal point in a numeric literal, Java assumes the literal is a double. Unfortunately, Java can't automatically convert a double to a float, because a float is smaller. Thus, the following won't compile:

```
float period = 99.0; // Does not compile
```

To force a numeric literal to be a float rather than a double, add the letter F to the end of the number, like this:

```
float period = 99.0F;
```

If you're using a mix of float and double types in your program, you may also want to explicitly designate your double literals as such by using a D suffix, like this:

```
float value1 = 199.33F;
double value2 = 200495.995D;
```

If you omit the suffix, D is assumed. As a result, you can usually omit the D suffix for double literals.

## The char type

The char type represents a single character from the Unicode character set. It's important to keep in mind that a character is not the same as a String; you find out about strings later in this chapter, in the section "Working with Strings." For now, just realize that a char variable can store just one character, not a sequence of characters, as a String can.

To assign a value to a char variable, you use a character literal, which is always enclosed in apostrophes rather than quotes. Here's an example:

```
char code = 'X';
```

Here the character X is assigned to the variable named code.

The following statement won't compile:

```
char code = "X"; // error -- should use apostrophes, not quotes
```

That's because quotation marks are used to mark Strings, not character constants.

You can also assign an integer value from 0 to 255 to a char variable, like this:

```
char cr = 013;
```

Here, the decimal value 13, which represents a carriage return, is assigned to the variable named cr.

Java uses a 16-bit fixed-length encoding scheme known as *UTF-16*, which is the most commonly used Unicode encoding scheme. The first 256 characters in the Unicode character set are the same as the characters of the ASCII character set, which is the most commonly used character set for computers with Western languages. (Strictly speaking, UTF-16 can encode 32-bit characters by using a pair of 16-bit sequences. But Java's char type can only handle the 16-bit UTF-16 codes.)

**TIP**

For more information about the Unicode character set, see the official Unicode website at https://home.unicode.org.

Character literals can also use special *escape sequences* to represent special characters. Table 4-2 lists the allowable escape sequences. These escape sequences let you create literals for characters that can't otherwise be typed within a character constant.

**TABLE 4-2** **Escape Sequences for Character Constants**

| Escape Sequence | Explanation |
| --- | --- |
| \b | Backspace |
| \t | Horizontal tab |
| \n | Line feed |
| \f | Form feed |
| \r | Carriage return |
| \" | Double quote |
| \' | Single quote |
| \\ | Backslash |

## The Boolean type

A Boolean type can have one of two values: true or false. Booleans are used to perform logical operations, most commonly to determine whether some condition is true. For example:

```
boolean enrolled = true;
boolean credited = false;
```

Here a variable named enrolled of type boolean is declared and initialized to a value of true, and another variable named credited of type boolean is declared and initialized to a value of false.

**WARNING**

In some languages, such as C or C++, integer values can be treated as Booleans, with 0 equal to false and any other value equal to true. Not so in Java. In Java, you can't convert between an integer type and a boolean type.

## Using wrapper classes

Every primitive type has a corresponding class defined in the Java API class library. This class is sometimes called a *wrapper class* because it wraps a primitive value with the object-oriented equivalent of pretty wrapping paper and a bow to make the primitive type look and behave like an object. Table 4-3 lists the wrapper classes for each of the eight primitive types.

**TABLE 4-3** ## Wrapper Classes for the Primitive Types

| Primitive Type | Wrapper Class |
| --- | --- |
| int | Integer |
| short | Short |
| long | Long |
| byte | Byte |
| float | Float |
| double | Double |
| char | Character |
| boolean | Boolean |

As you find out later in this chapter, you can use these wrapper classes to convert primitive values to strings, and vice versa.

## Using reference types

In Chapter 10, you're introduced to some of the basic concepts of object-oriented programming. In particular, you see how all Java programs are made up of one or more classes, and how to use classes to create objects. In this section, we show how you can create variables that work with objects created from classes.

To start, a *reference type* is a type that's based on a class rather than on one of the primitive types that are built into the Java language. A reference type can be based on a class that's provided as part of the Java API class library or on a class that you write yourself. Either way, when you create an object from a class, Java allocates however much memory the object requires to store the object. Then, if you assign the object to a variable, the variable is actually assigned a *reference* to the object, not the object itself. This reference is the address of the memory location where the object is stored.

Suppose that you're writing a game program that involves balls, and you create a class named Ball that defines the behavior of a ball. To declare a variable that can refer to a Ball object, you use a statement like this:

```
Ball b;
```

Here, the variable b is a variable of type Ball.

To create a new instance of an object from a class, use the new keyword along with the class name. This second reference to the class name is actually a call to a special routine of the class called a *constructor*. The constructor is responsible for initializing the new object. Here's a statement that declares a variable of type Ball, calls the Ball class constructor to create a new Ball object, and assigns a reference to the Ball object to the variable:

```
Ball b = new Ball();
```

REMEMBER

One of the key concepts in working with reference types is the fact that a variable of a particular type doesn't actually contain an object of that type. Instead, it contains a reference to an object of the correct type. An important side effect is that two variables can refer to the same object.

Consider these statements:

```
Ball b1 = new Ball();
Ball b2 = b1;
```

Here we've declared two `Ball` variables, named b1 and b2, but we've created only one `Ball` object. In the first statement, the `Ball` object is created, and b1 is assigned a reference to it. Then, in the second statement, the variable b2 is assigned a reference to the same object that's referenced by b1. As a result, both b1 and b2 refer to the same `Ball` object.

If you use one of these variables to change some aspect of the ball, the change is visible to the ball no matter which variable you use. Suppose that the `Ball` class has a method called setSpeed that lets you set the speed of the ball to any int value and a getSpeed method that returns an integer value that reflects the ball's current speed. Now consider these statements:

```
b1.setSpeed(50);
b2.setSpeed(100);
int speed = b1.getSpeed();
```

When these statements complete, is the value of the speed variable 50 or 100? The correct answer is 100. Because b1 and b2 refer to the same `Ball` object, changing the speed by using b2 affects b1 as well.

This is one of the most confusing aspects of programming with an object-oriented language such as Java, so don't feel bad if you get tripped up from time to time.

## Working with Strings

A *String* is a sequence of text characters, such as the message "Hello, World!" displayed by the HelloApp program illustrated in this chapter and the preceding chapter. In Java, strings are an interesting breed. Java doesn't define strings as a primitive type. Instead, strings are a *reference type* defined by the Java API String class. The Java language does have some built-in features for working with strings. In some cases, these features make strings appear to be primitive types rather than reference types.

The following sections present just the bare essentials of working with strings so that you can incorporate simple strings into your programs.

# Declaring and initializing strings

Strings are declared and initialized much like primitive types. In fact, the only difference you may notice at first is that the word String is capitalized, unlike the keywords for the primitive types, such as int and double. That's because String isn't a keyword. Instead, it's the name of the Java API class that provides for string objects.

The following statements define and initialize a string variable:

```
String s;
s = "Hello, World!";
```

Here a variable named s of type String is declared and initialized with the *string literal* "Hello, World!". Notice that string literals are enclosed in quotation marks, not apostrophes. Apostrophes are used for character literals, which are different from string literals.

Like any variable declaration, a string declaration can include an initializer. Thus you can declare and initialize a string variable in one statement, like this:

```
String s = "Hello, World!";
```

**TIP**

Class variables and instance variables are automatically initialized to empty strings, but local variables aren't. To initialize a local string variable to an empty string, use a statement like this:

```
String s = "";
```

# Combining strings

Combine two strings by using the plus sign (+) as a *concatenation operator*. (In Java-speak, combining strings is called *concatenation*.) The following statement combines the value of two string variables to create a third string:

```
String hello = "Hello, ";
String world = "World!";
String greeting = hello + world;
```

The final value of the greeting variable is "Hello, World!".

**TIP**

When Java concatenates strings, it doesn't insert any blank spaces between the strings. Thus, if you want to combine two strings and have a space appear between them, make sure that the first string ends with a space or the second string begins with a space. (In the preceding example, the first string ends with a space.)

Alternatively, you can concatenate a string literal along with the string variables. For example:

```
String hello = "Hello";
String world = "World!";
String greeting = hello + ", " + world;
```

Here the comma and the space that appear between the words Hello and World are inserted as a string literal.

Concatenation is one of the most commonly used string-handling techniques, so you see plenty of examples in this book. In fact, we've already used concatenation once in this chapter. Earlier, we showed you a program that included the following line:

```
System.out.println("The value of i is " + i);
```

Here the `println` method of the `System.out` object prints the string that's created when the literal `"The value of i is "` is concatenated with the value of the `i` variable.

## Converting primitives to strings

Because string concatenation lets you combine two or more string values, and because primitive types such as int and double are *not* string types, you may be wondering how the last example in the preceding section can work. In other words, how can Java concatenate the string literal `"The value of i is "` with the integer value of `i` in this statement?

```
System.out.println("The value of i is " + i);
```

The answer is that Java automatically converts primitive values to string values whenever you use a primitive value in a concatenation.

Be careful here: Java can confuse you about when the numbers are converted to strings in the course of evaluating the complete expression. Consider this admittedly far-fetched example:

```
int i = 2;
System.out.println(i + i + " equals four.");
```

This prints the following on the console:

```
4 equals four.
```

Here, the first plus sign indicates the addition of two `int` variables rather than concatenation. For the second plus sign, the resulting `int` answer is converted to a string and concatenated with `" equals four."`

You can explicitly convert a primitive value to a string by using the `toString` method of the primitive type's wrapper class. To convert the `int` variable x to a string, for example, you use this statement:

```
String s = Integer.toString(x);
```

In the next chapter, you discover how to use a special class called the `NumberFormat` class to convert primitive types to strings while applying various types of formatting to the value, such as adding commas, currency symbols, or percentage marks.

## Converting strings to primitives

Converting a primitive value to a string value is pretty easy. Going the other way — converting a string value to a primitive — is a little more complex, because it doesn't always work. If a string contains the value 10, for example, you can easily convert it to an integer. But if the string contains `thirty-two`, you can't.

To convert a string to a primitive type, you use a `parse` method of the appropriate wrapper class, as listed in Table 4-4. To convert a string value to an integer, you use statements like this:

```
String s = "10";
int x = Integer.parseInt(s);
```

TABLE 4-4
## Methods That Convert Strings to Numeric Primitive Types

| Wrapper | parse Method | Example |
|---------|--------------|---------|
| Integer | parseInt(String) | int x = Integer.parseInt("100"); |
| Short | parseShort(String) | short x = Short.parseShort("100"); |
| Long | parseLong(String) | long x = Long.parseLong("100"); |
| Byte | parseByte(String) | byte x = Byte.parseByte("100"); |
| Float | parseFloat(String) | float x = Float.parseFloat("19.95"); |
| Double | parseDouble(String) | double x = Double.parseDouble("19.95"); |
| Character | (none) | |
| Boolean | parseBoolean (String) | boolean x = Boolean.parseBoolean("true"); |

# Understanding Scope

The *scope* of a variable refers to which parts of a class the variable exists in. In the simplest terms, every variable exists only within the block in which the variable is declared, as well as any blocks that are contained within that block. That's why class variables, which are declared in the class body, can be accessed by any methods defined by the class, but local variables defined within a method can be accessed only by the method in which they are defined.

REMEMBER

In Java, a *block* is marked by a matching pair of braces. Java has many kinds of blocks, including class bodies, method bodies, and block statements that belong to statements such as if or for statements. But in each case, a block marks the scope boundaries for the variables declared within it.

The program in Listing 4-1 can help clarify the scope of class and local variables.

---

**LISTING 4-1:** **A Program That Demonstrates Scope for Class and Local Variables**

```
public class ScopeApp
{                                                           →2
    static int x;
    public static void main(String[] args)
    {
        x = 5;
        System.out.println("main: x = " + x);
        myMethod();
    }
    public static void myMethod()
    {
        int y;                                              →12
        y = 10;
        if (y == x + 5)
{                                                           →15
        int z;
        z = 15;
        System.out.println("myMethod: z = " + z);
}                                                           →19
        System.out.println("myMethod: x = " + x);
        System.out.println("myMethod: y = " + y);
}                                                           →22
}                                                           →23
```

---

The following paragraphs explain the scope of each of the variables used in this class:

→2:  The variable x is a class variable. Its scope begins in line 2 and ends in line 23. As a result, both the main method and the myMethod method can access it.

→12: The variable y is a local variable that's declared in line 12 and initialized in the next line. As a result, its scope begins in line 12 and ends in line 22, which marks the end of the body of the myMethod method.

→15: The line marks the beginning of an if block that controls the scope of variable z.

→19: This line marks the end of the scope of variable z.

→22: This line marks the end of the myMethod method body and, therefore, the end of the scope of variable y.

When you run this program, you'll get the following output:

```
main: x = 5
myMethod: z = 15
myMethod: x = 5
myMethod: y = 10
```

IN THIS CHAPTER

» **Dealing with operators, such as +, –, \*, and /**

» **Creating finely crafted expressions**

» **Using the** Math **class**

» **Formatting your numbers**

# Chapter **5**

# Working with Numbers and Expressions

I n Chapter 4, you discover the various primitive numeric types that are supported by Java. In this chapter, you build on that knowledge by doing basic operations with numbers. Much of this chapter focuses on the complex topic of *expressions*, which combine numbers with operators to perform calculations. This chapter also covers performing advanced calculations using the Math class and techniques for formatting numbers when you display them.

## Working with Arithmetic Operators

An *operator* is a special symbol or keyword that's used to designate a mathematical operation or some other type of operation that can be performed on one or more values, called *operands*. In all, Java has about 40 operators. This chapter focuses on the operators that do arithmetic. These *arithmetic operators* — seven of them in all, summarized in Table 5-1 — perform basic arithmetic operations, such as addition, subtraction, multiplication, and division.

## TABLE 5-1    Java's Arithmetic Operators

| Operator | Description |
|----------|-------------|
| + | Addition; also used as a unary operator to indicate a positive number |
| – | Subtraction; also used as a unary operator to indicate a negative number |
| * | Multiplication |
| / | Division |
| % | Remainder (Modulus) |
| ++ | Increment |
| –– | Decrement |

The following section of code can help clarify how these operators work for int types:

```
int a = 32, b = 5;
int c = a + b; // c is 37
int d = a - b; // d is 27
int e = a * b; // e is 160
int f = a / b; // f is 6 (32 / 5 is 6 remainder 2)
int g = a % b; // g is 2 (32 / 5 is 6 remainder 2)
a++; // a is now 33
b--; // b is now 4
```

Notice that for division, the result is truncated. Thus 32 / 5 returns 6, not 6.4.

Here's how the operators work for double values:

```
double x = 5.5, y = 2.0;
double m = x + y; // m is 7.5
double n = x - y; // n is 3.5
double o = x * y; // o is 11.0
double p = x / y; // p is 2.75
double q = x % y; // q is 1.5
x++; // x is now 6.5
y--; // y is now 1.0
```

# Using Compound Assignment Operators

A *compound assignment operator* is an operator that performs a calculation and an assignment at the same time. All of Java's binary arithmetic operators (that is, the ones that work on two operands) have equivalent compound assignment operators, which Table 5-2 lists.

**TABLE 5-2** Compound Assignment Operators

| Operator | Description |
|----------|-------------|
| += | Addition and assignment |
| -= | Subtraction and assignment |
| *= | Multiplication and assignment |
| /= | Division and assignment |
| %= | Remainder and assignment |

The statement

```
a += 10;
```

is equivalent to

```
a = a + 10;
```

Also, the statement

```
z *=2;
```

is equivalent to

```
z = z * 2;
```

# Using the Math Class

Java's built-in operators are useful, but they don't come anywhere near providing all the mathematical needs of most Java programmers. That's where the Math class comes in. It includes a bevy of built-in methods that perform a wide variety of mathematical calculations, from basic functions such as calculating an absolute value or a square root to trigonometry functions such as sin and cos (sine and cosine), to practical functions such as rounding numbers or generating random numbers.

The following sections describe the most useful methods of the Math class.

## Using constants of the Math class

The Math class defines two constants that are useful for many mathematical calculations. Table 5-3 lists these constants.

**TABLE 5-3 Constants of the Math Class**

| Constant | What It Is | Value |
|----------|-----------|-------|
| PI | The constant pi ($\pi$), the ratio of a circle's radius and diameter | 3.141592653589793 |
| E | The base of natural logarithms | 2.718281828459045 |

Note that these constants are only approximate values, because both $\pi$ and $e$ are irrational numbers.

The program shown in Listing 5-1 illustrates a typical use of the constant PI. Here, the user is asked to enter the radius of a circle. Then the program calculates the area of the circle in line 11. (The parentheses aren't really required in the expression in this statement, but they help clarify that the expression is the Java equivalent to the formula for the area of a circle, $\pi r^2$.)

Here's the console output for a typical execution of this program, in which the user entered 5 as the radius of the circle:

```
Welcome to the circle area calculator.
Enter the radius of your circle: 5
The area is 78.53981633974483
```

LISTING 5-1: **The Circle Area Calculator**

```java
import java.util.Scanner;
public class CircleAreaApp
{
    static Scanner sc = new Scanner(System.in);
    public static void main(String[] args)
    {
        System.out.println(
            "Welcome to the circle area calculator.");
        System.out.print("Enter the radius of your
circle: ");
        double r = sc.nextDouble();
        double area = Math.PI * (r * r);              →11
        System.out.println("The area is " + area);
    }
}
```

# Working with mathematical functions

Table 5-4 lists the basic mathematical functions that are provided by the Math class. As you can see, you can use these functions to calculate such things as the absolute value of a number, the minimum and maximum of two values, square roots, powers, and logarithms.

**TABLE 5-4** **Commonly Used Mathematical Functions Provided by the Math Class**

| Method | Explanation |
|---|---|
| abs(argument) | Returns the absolute value of the argument. The argument can be an int, long, float, or double. The return value is the same type as the argument. |
| cbrt(argument) | Returns the cube root of the argument. The argument and return value are doubles. |
| exp(argument) | Returns e raised to the power of the argument. The argument and the return value are doubles. |
| hypot(arg1, arg2) | Returns the hypotenuse of a right triangle calculated according to the Pythagorean theorem — $\sqrt{x^2 + y^2}$. The argument and the return values are doubles. |

*(continued)*

**TABLE 5-4** *(continued)*

| Method | Explanation |
|---|---|
| log(argument) | Returns the natural logarithm (base *e*) of the argument. The argument and the return value are doubles. |
| log10(argument) | Returns the base 10 logarithm of the argument. The argument and the return value are doubles. |
| max(arg1, arg2) | Returns the larger of the two arguments. The arguments can be int, long, float, or double. The return type is the same type as the arguments. |
| min(arg1, arg2) | Returns the smaller of the two arguments. The arguments can be int, long, float, or double. The return type is the same type as the arguments. |
| pow(arg1, arg2) | Returns the value of the first argument raised to the power of the second argument. Both arguments and the return value are doubles. |
| random() | Returns a random number that's greater than or equal to 0.0 but less than 1.0. This method doesn't accept an argument, but the return value is a double. |
| signum(argument) | Returns a number that represents the sign of the argument: –1.0 if the argument is negative, 0.0 if the argument is zero, and 1.0 if the argument is positive. The argument can be a double or a float. The return value is the same type as the argument. |
| sqrt(argument) | Returns the square root of the argument. The argument and return value are doubles. |

The program shown in Listing 5-2 demonstrates each of these methods. When run, it produces output similar to this:

```
abs(b) = 50
cbrt(x) = 2.924017738212866
exp(y) = 54.598150033144236
hypot(y,z)= 5.0
log(y) = 1.0986122886681098
log10(y) = 0.47712125471966244
max(a, b) = 100
min(a, b) = -50
pow(a, c) = 1000000.0
```

```
random() = 0.8536014557793756
signum(b) = -1.0
sqrt(x) = 1.7320508075688772
```

LISTING 5-2: **A Program That Uses the Mathematical Methods of the Math Class**

```java
public class MathFunctionsApp
{
    public static void main(String[] args)
    {
        int a = 100;
        int b = -50;
        int c = 3;
        double x = 25.0;
        double y = 3.0;
        double z = 4.0;

        System.out.println("abs(b) = " + Math.abs(b));
        System.out.println("cbrt(x) = " +
Math.cbrt(x));
        System.out.println("exp(y) = " + Math.exp(z));
        System.out.println("hypot(y,z) = " + Math.
hypot(y,z));
        System.out.println("log(y) = " + Math.log(y));
        System.out.println("log10(y) = " + Math.
log10(y));
        System.out.println("max(a, b) = " + Math.
max(a, b));
        System.out.println("min(a, b) = " + Math.
min(a, b));
        System.out.println("pow(a, c) = " + Math.
pow(a, c));
        System.out.println("random() = " + Math.
random());
        System.out.println("signum(b) = " + Math.
signum(b));
        System.out.println("sqrt(x) = " +
Math.sqrt(y));
    }
}
```

# Creating random numbers

Sooner or later, you're going to want to write programs that play simple games. Almost all games have some element of chance built into them, so you need a way to create computer programs that don't work exactly the same every time you run them. The easiest way to do that is to use the random method of the Math class, which Table 5-4 lists earlier in this section, along with the other basic mathematical functions of the Math class.

The random method generates a random double value between 0.0 (inclusive, meaning that it could be 0.0) and 1.0 (exclusive, meaning that it can't be 1.0). Most computer applications that need random values, however, need random integers between some arbitrary low value (usually 1, but not always) and some arbitrary high value. A program that plays dice needs random numbers between 1 and 6, whereas a program that deals cards needs random numbers between 1 and 52 (53 if a joker is used).

As a result, you need a Java expression that converts the double value returned by the random function to an int value within the range your program calls for. The following code shows how to do this, with the values set to 1 and 6 for a dice-playing game:

```
int low = 1; // the lowest value in the range
int high = 6; // the highest value in the range
int rnd = (int)(Math.random() * (high - low + 1)) + low;
```

This expression is a little complicated, so we show you how it's evaluated step by step:

1. The Math.Random method is called to get a random double value. This value is greater than 0.0 but less than 1.0.

2. The random value is multiplied by the high end of the range minus the low end, plus 1. In this example, the high end is 6 and the low end is 1, so you now have a random number that's greater than or equal to 0.0 but less than 6.0. (It could be 5.99999999999999, but it never is 6.0.)

3. This value is converted to an integer by the (int) cast. Now you have an integer that's 0, 1, 2, 3, 4, or 5.

**4.** The low value in the range is added to the random number. Assuming that low is 1, the random number is now 1, 2, 3, 4, 5, or 6. That's just what you want: a random number between 1 and 6.

To give you an idea of how this random-number calculation works, Listing 5-3 shows a program that places this calculation in a method called randomInt and then calls it to simulate 100 dice rolls. The randomInt method accepts two parameters representing the low and high ends of the range, and it returns a random integer within the range. In the main method of this program, the randomInt method is called 100 times, and each random number is printed by a call to System.out.print.

The console output for this program looks like this:

```
Here are 100 random rolls of the dice:
4 1 1 6 1 2 6 6 6 6 5 5 5 4 5 4 4 1 3 6 1 3 1 4 4 3 3 3 5 6 5 6 6 3
   5 2 2 6 3 3
4 1 2 2 4 2 2 4 1 4 3 6 5 5 4 4 2 4 1 3 5 2 1 3 3 5 4 1 6 3 1 6 5 2
   6 6 3 5 4 5
2 5 4 5 3 1 4 2 5 2 1 4 4 4 6 6 4 6 3 3
```

Every time you run this program, however, you see a different sequence of 100 numbers.

The program in Listing 5-3 uses several Java features that you haven't seen yet.

LISTING 5-3: **Rolling the Dice**

```java
public class DiceApp
{
    public static void main(String[] args)
    {
        int roll;
        String msg = "Here are 100 random rolls of
the dice:";
        System.out.println(msg);
        for (int i=0; i<100; i++)                      →8
        {
            roll = randomInt(1, 6);                     →10
```

```
            System.out.print(roll + " ");          →11
        }
        System.out.println();
    }

    public static int randomInt(int low, int high)   →16
    {
        int result = (int)(Math.random()             →18
            * (high - low + 1)) + low;
        return result;                               →20
    }
}
```

The following paragraphs explain how the program works.

→8:  The for statement causes the statements in its body
     (lines 10 and 11) to be executed 100 times. Don't worry
     about how this statement works for now; you find out
     about it in Chapter 7.

→10: This statement calls the randomInt method, specifying 1
     and 6 as the range for the random integer to generate.
     The resulting random number is assigned to the
     roll variable.

→11: The System.out.print method is used to print the
     random number followed by a space. Because this
     statement calls the print method rather than the
     println method, the random numbers are printed on
     the same line rather than on separate lines.

→16: The declaration for the randomInt method indicates that
     the method returns an int value and accepts two int
     arguments: one named low and the other named high.

→18: This expression converts the random double value to an
     integer between low and high.

→20: The return statement sends the random number back
     to the statement that called the randomInt method.

# Rounding functions

The Math class has four methods that round or truncate float or
double values. Table 5-5 lists these methods.

## TABLE 5-5 Rounding Functions Provided by the Math Class

| Method | Explanation |
|---|---|
| ceil(argument) | Returns the smallest double value that is an integer and is greater than or equal to the value of the argument. |
| floor(argument) | Returns the largest double value that is an integer and is less than or equal to the value of the argument. |
| rint(argument) | Returns the double value that is an integer and is closest to the value of the argument. If two integer values are equally close, it returns the one that is even. If the argument is already an integer, it returns the argument value. |
| round(argument) | Returns the integer that is closest to the argument. If the argument is a double, it returns a long. If the argument is a float, it returns an int. |

Listing 5-4 shows a program that uses each of the four methods to round three double values: 29.4, 93.5, and –19.3. Here's the output from this program:

```
round(x) = 29
round(y) = 94
round(z) = -19

ceil(x) = 30.0
ceil(y) = 94.0
ceil(z) = -19.0

floor(x) = 29.0
floor(y) = 93.0
floor(z) = -20.0

rint(x) = 29.0
rint(y) = 94.0
rint(z) = -19.0
```

Note that each of the four methods produces a different result for at least one of the values:

>> All the methods except ceil return 29.0 (or 29) for the value 29.4. ceil returns 30.0, which is the smallest integer that's greater than 29.4.

>> All the methods except floor return 94.0 (or 94) for the value 93.5. floor returns 93.0 because that's the largest integer that's less than 93.5. rint returns 94.0 because it's an even number, and 93.5 is midway between 93.0 and 94.0.

>> All the methods except floor return -19.0 (or -19) for -19.3. floor returns -20 because -20 is the largest integer that's less than -19.3.

---

**LISTING 5-4:** **Program That Uses the Rounding Methods of the Math Class**

```
public class RoundingApp
{
    public static void main(String[] args)
    {
        double x = 29.4;
        double y = 93.5;
        double z = -19.3;

        System.out.println("round(x) = " + Math.
round(x));
        System.out.println("round(y) = " + Math.
round(y));
        System.out.println("round(z) = " + Math.
round(z));
        System.out.println();

        System.out.println("ceil(x) = " +
Math.ceil(x));
        System.out.println("ceil(y) = " +
Math.ceil(y));
        System.out.println("ceil(z) = " +
Math.ceil(z));
        System.out.println();
```

```
        System.out.println("floor(x) = " + Math.
floor(x));
        System.out.println("floor(y) = " + Math.
floor(y));
        System.out.println("floor(z) = " + Math.
floor(z));
        System.out.println();

        System.out.println("rint(x) = " +
Math.rint(x));
        System.out.println("rint(y) = " +
Math.rint(y));
        System.out.println("rint(z) = " +
Math.rint(z));
    }
}
```

# Formatting Numbers

In many cases, you want to format your numbers before you print them — to add commas to large values and limit the number of decimal places printed, for example. Or, if a number represents a monetary amount, you may want to add a dollar sign (or whatever currency symbol is appropriate for your locale). To do that, you can use the NumberFormat class. Table 5-6 lists the NumberFormat class methods.

The procedure for using the NumberFormat class to format numbers takes a little getting used to. First, you must call one of the static get*Xxx*Instance methods to create a NumberFormat object that can format numbers in a particular way. Then, if you want, you can call the setMinimumFractionDigits or setMaximumFractionDigits method to set the number of decimal digits to be displayed. Finally, you call that object's format method to actually format a number.

Note that the NumberFormat class is in the java.text package, so you must include the following import statement at the beginning of any class that uses NumberFormat:

```
import java.text.NumberFormat;
```

**TABLE 5-6** Methods of the NumberFormat Class

| Method | Explanation |
| --- | --- |
| getCurrencyInstance() | A static method that returns a NumberFormat object that formats currency values |
| getPercentInstance() | A static method that returns a NumberFormat object that formats percentages |
| getNumberInstance() | A static method that returns a NumberFormat object that formats basic numbers |
| format(number) | Returns a string that contains the formatted number |
| setMinimumFractionDigits(int) | Sets the minimum number of digits to display to the right of the decimal point |
| setMaximumFractionDigits(int) | Sets the maximum number of digits to display to the right of the decimal point |

Here's an example that uses the NumberFormat class to format a double value as currency:

```
double salesTax = 2.426;
NumberFormat cf = NumberFormat.getCurrencyInstance();
System.out.println(cf.format(salesTax));
```

When you run this code, the following line is printed to the console:

```
$2.43
```

Note that the currency format rounds the value from 2.426 to 2.43.

Here's an example that formats a number by using the general number format, with exactly three decimal places:

```
double x = 19923.3288;
NumberFormat nf = NumberFormat.getNumberInstance();
nf.setMinimumFractionDigits(3);
nf.setMaximumFractionDigits(3);
System.out.println(nf.format(x));
```

When you run this code, the following line is printed:

```
19,923.329
```

Here the number is formatted with a comma and the value is rounded to three places.

Here's an example that uses the percentage format:

```
double grade = .92;
NumberFormat pf = NumberFormat.getPercentInstance();
System.out.println(pf.format(grade));
```

When you run this code, the following line is printed:

```
92%
```

IN THIS CHAPTER

» **Boring into Boolean expressions for fun and profit**

» **Focusing on your basic, run-of-the-mill if statement**

» **Looking at else clauses and else-if statements**

» **Considering logical operators**

» **Using the switch statement**

# Chapter **6**

# Making Choices

S o far in this book, all the programs have run straight through from start to finish without making any decisions along the way. In this chapter, you discover two Java statements that let you create some variety in your programs. The if statement lets you execute a statement or a block of statements only if some conditional test turns out to be true. And the switch statement lets you execute one of several blocks of statements depending on the value of an integer variable.

## Using Simple Boolean Expressions

All if statements, as well as several of the other control statements that we describe in Chapter 7 (while, do, and for), use Boolean expressions to determine whether to execute or skip a statement (or a block of statements). A *Boolean expression* is a Java expression that, when evaluated, returns a *Boolean value:* true or false.

As you discover later in this chapter, Boolean expressions can be very complicated. Most of the time, however, you use simple expressions that compare the value of a variable with the value of some other variable, a literal, or perhaps a simple arithmetic expression. This comparison uses one of the *relational operators* listed in Table 6-1. All these operators are *binary operators*, which means that they work on two operands.

**TABLE 6-1  Relational Operators**

| Operator | Description |
|---|---|
| == | Returns true if the expression on the left evaluates to the same value as the expression on the right |
| != | Returns true if the expression on the left does not evaluate to the same value as the expression on the right |
| < | Returns true if the expression on the left evaluates to a value that is less than the value of the expression on the right |
| <= | Returns true if the expression on the left evaluates to a value that is less than or equal to the expression on the right |
| > | Returns true if the expression on the left evaluates to a value that is greater than the value of the expression on the right |
| >= | Returns true if the expression on the left evaluates to a value that is greater than or equal to the expression on the right |

A basic Java Boolean expression has this form:

```
expression relational-operator expression
```

Java evaluates a Boolean expression by first evaluating the expression on the left, then evaluating the expression on the right, and finally applying the relational operator to determine whether the entire expression evaluates to true or false.

Here are some simple examples of relational expressions. For each example, assume that the following statements were used to declare and initialize the variables:

```
int i = 5;
int j = 10;
int k = 15;
double x = 5.0;
double y = 7.5;
double z = 12.3;
```

Here are the sample expressions, along with their results (based on the values supplied):

| Expression | Value | Explanation |
|---|---|---|
| i == 5 | true | The value of i is 5. |
| i == 10 | false | The value of i is not 10. |
| i == j | false | i is 5, and j is 10, so they are not equal. |
| i == j - 5 | true | i is 5, and j - 5 is 5. |
| i > 1 | true | i is 5, which is greater than 1. |
| j == i * 2 | true | j is 10, and i is 5, so i * 2 is also 10. |
| x == i | true | Casting allows the comparison, and 5.0 is equal to 5. |
| k < z | false | Casting allows the comparison, and 15 is greater than 12.3. |
| i * 2 < y | false | i * 2 is 10, which is not less than 7.5. |

**WARNING**

Note that the relational operator that tests for equality is two equal signs in a row (==). A single equal sign is the assignment operator. When you're first learning Java, you may find yourself typing the assignment operator when you mean the equals operator, like this:

```
if (i = 5)
```

Oops. But Java won't let you get away with this, so you have to correct your mistake and recompile the program. At first, doing so seems like a nuisance. The more you work with Java, the more you come to appreciate that comparison and assignment are two different things, and it's best that a single operator (=) isn't overloaded with both functions.

# Using if Statements

The if statement is one of the most important statements in any programming language, and Java is no exception. The following sections describe the ins and outs of using the various forms of Java's powerful if statement.

## Simple if statements

In its most basic form, an if statement lets you execute a single statement or a block of statements only if a Boolean expression evaluates to true. The basic form of the if statement looks like this:

```
if (boolean-expression)
    statement
```

Note that the Boolean expression must be enclosed in parentheses. Also, if you use only a single statement, it must end with a semicolon. But the statement can also be a statement block enclosed by braces. In that case, each statement within the block needs a semicolon, but the block itself doesn't.

Here's an example of a typical if statement:

```
double commissionRate = 0.0;
if (salesTotal > 10000.0)
    commissionRate = 0.05;
```

In this example, a variable named commissionRate is initialized to 0.0 and then set to 0.05 if salesTotal is greater than 10000.0.

**TIP**

Indenting the statement under the if statement is customary because it makes the structure of your code more obvious. It isn't necessary, but it's always a good idea.

Here's an example that uses a block rather than a single statement:

```
double commissionRate = 0.0;

if (salesTotal > 10000.0)
{
    commissionRate = 0.05;
    commission = salesTotal * commissionRate;
}
```

In this example, the two statements within the braces are executed if sales Total is greater than $10,000. Otherwise neither statement is executed.

## if-else statements

An if-else statement adds an additional element to a basic if statement: a statement or block that's executed if the Boolean expression is not true. Its basic format is

```
if (boolean-expression)
    statement
else
    statement
```

Here's an example:

```
double commissionRate;

if (salesTotal > 10000.0)
    commissionRate = 0.05;
else
    commissionRate = 0.02;
```

In this example, the commission rate is set to 5 percent if the sales total is greater than $10,000. If the sales total is less than or equal to $10,000, the commission rate is set to 2 percent.

You can use blocks for either or both of the statements in an if-else statement. Here's an if-else statement in which both statements are blocks:

```
double commissionRate;

if (salesTotal > 10000.0)
{
    commissionRate = 0.05;
    level2Count++;
}
else
{
    commissionRate = 0.02;
    level1Count++;
}
```

# else-if statements

A common pattern for nested if statements is to have a series of if-else statements with another if-else statement in each else part:

```
if (expression-1)
    statement-1
else if (expression-2)
    statement-2
else if (expression-3)
    statement-3
```

These statements are sometimes called *else-if statements,* although that term is unofficial. Officially, all that's going on is that the statement in the else part happens to be another if statement — so this statement is just a type of a nested if statement. It's an especially useful form of nesting, however.

Suppose that you want to assign four commission rates based on the sales total, according to this table:

| Sales | Commission |
|---|---|
| $10,000 and above | 5% |
| $5,000 to $9,999 | 3.5% |
| $1,000 to $4,999 | 2% |
| Under $1,000 | 0% |

You can easily implement a series of else-if statements:

```
if (salesTotal >= 10000.0)
    commissionRate = 0.05;
else if (salesTotal >= 5000.0)
    commissionRate = 0.035;
else if (salesTotal >= 1000.0)
    commissionRate = 0.02;
else
    commissionRate = 0.0;
```

You have to think through carefully how you set up these else-if statements. At first glance, for example, this sequence looks as though it might work:

```
if (salesTotal > 0.0)
    commissionRate = 0.0;
else if (salesTotal >= 1000.0)
    commissionRate = 0.02;
else if (salesTotal >= 5000.0)
    commissionRate = 0.035;
else if (salesTotal >= 10000.0)
    commissionRate = 0.05;
```

Nice try, but this scenario won't work. These if statements always set the commission rate to 0 percent because the Boolean expression in the first if statement always tests true (assuming that the salesTotal isn't zero or negative — and if it is, none of the other if statements matter). As a result, none of the other if statements are ever evaluated.

# Using Mr. Spock's Favorite Operators (Logical Ones, of Course)

A *logical operator* (sometimes called a *Boolean operator*) is an operator that returns a Boolean result that's based on the Boolean result of one or two other expressions. Expressions that use logical operators are sometimes called *compound expressions* because the effect of the logical operators is to let you combine two or more condition tests into a single expression. Table 6-2 lists the logical operators.

The following sections describe most of these operators in excruciating detail.

## Using the ! operator

The simplest of the logical operators is *Not* (!). Technically, it's a *unary* prefix operator, which means that you use it with one operand, and you code it immediately in front of that operand. (Technically, this operator is called the *complement operator*, not the *Not* operator. But in real life, most people call it *Not*. And many programmers call it *bang*.)

**TABLE 6-2  Logical Operators**

| Operator | Name | Type | Description |
|---|---|---|---|
| ! | Not | Unary | Returns true if the operand to the right evaluates to false. Returns false if the operand to the right is true. |
| & | And | Binary | Returns true if both of the operands evaluate to true. Both operands are evaluated before the And operator is applied. |
| \| | Or | Binary | Returns true if at least one of the operands evaluates to true. Both operands are evaluated before the Or operator is applied. |
| ^ | Xor | Binary | Returns true if one — and only one — of the operands evaluates to true. Returns false if both operands evaluate to true or if both operands evaluate to false. |
| && | Conditional And | Binary | Same as &, but if the operand on the left returns false, returns false without evaluating the operand on the right. |
| \|\| | Conditional Or | Binary | Same as \|, but if the operand on the left returns true, returns true without evaluating the operand on the right. |

The Not operator reverses the value of a Boolean expression. Thus, if the expression is true, Not changes it to false. If the expression is false, Not changes it to true.

Here's an example:

```
!(i == 4)
```

This expression evaluates to true if i is any value other than 4. If i is 4, it evaluates to false. It works by first evaluating the expression (i == 4). Then it reverses the result of that evaluation.

**TIP**

Don't confuse the Not logical operator (!) with the Not Equals relational operator (!=). Although these operators are sometimes used in similar ways, the Not operator is more general. We could have written the preceding example like this:

```
i != 4
```

The result is the same. The Not operator can be applied to any expression that returns a `true-false` result, however, not just to an equality test.

You must almost always enclose the expression that the ! operator is applied to in parentheses. Consider this expression:

```
! i == 4
```

Assuming that i is an integer variable, the compiler doesn't allow this expression because it looks like you're trying to apply the ! operator to the variable, not to the result of the comparison. A quick set of parentheses solves the problem:

```
!(i == 4)
```

## Using the & and && operators

The & and && operators combine two Boolean expressions and return `true` only if both expressions are `true`. This type of operation is called an *And operation,* because the first expression and the second expression must be `true` for the And operator to return `true`.

Suppose that the sales commission rate should be 2.5% if the sales class is 1 and the sales total is $10,000 or more. You could perform this test with two separate if statements (as we did earlier in this chapter), or you could combine the tests into one if statement:

```
if ((salesClass == 1) & (salesTotal >= 10000.0))
    commissionRate = 0.025;
```

Here the expressions (salesClass == 1) and (salesTotal >= 10000.0) are evaluated separately. Then the & operator compares the results. If they're both `true`, the & operator returns `true`. If one is `false` or both are `false`, the & operator returns `false`.

Notice that we use parentheses liberally to clarify where one expression ends and another begins. Using parentheses isn't always necessary, but when you use logical operators, we suggest that you always use parentheses to clearly identify the expressions being compared.

The && operator is similar to the & operator, but it leverages your knowledge of logic a bit more. Because both expressions compared by the & operator must be true for the entire expression to be true, there's no reason to evaluate the second expression if the first one returns false. The & operator isn't aware of this fact, so it blindly evaluates both expressions before determining the results. The && operator is smart enough to stop when it knows what the outcome is.

As a result, almost always use && instead of &. Here's the preceding example, and this time it's coded smartly with &&:

```
if ((salesClass == 1) && (salesTotal >= 10000.0))
    commissionRate = 0.025;
```

Why do we say you should *almost* always use &&? Because sometimes the expressions themselves have side effects that are important. The second expression might involve a method call that updates a database, for example, and you want the database to be updated whether the first expression evaluates to true or to false. In that case, you want to use & instead of && to ensure that both expressions get evaluated.

Relying on the side effects of expressions can be risky — and you can almost always find a better way to write your code to avert the side effects. In other words, placing an important call to a database-update method inside a compound expression that's buried in an if statement probably isn't a good idea.

## Using the | and || operators

The | and || operators are called *Or operators* because they return true if the first expression is true or if the second expression is true. They also return true if both expressions are true. (You find the | symbol on your keyboard just above the Enter key.)

Suppose that sales representatives get no commission if total sales are less than $1,000 or if the sales class is 3. You could do that with two separate if statements:

```
if (salesTotal < 1000.0)
    commissionRate = 0.0;
if (salesClass == 3)
    commissionRate = 0.0;
```

With an Or operator, however, you can do the same thing with a compound condition:

```
if ((salesTotal < 1000.0) | (salesClass == 3))
    commissionRate = 0.0;
```

To evaluate the expression for this if statement, Java first evaluates the expressions on either side of the | operator. Then, if at least one of these expressions is true, the whole expression is true. Otherwise the expression is false.

In most cases, you should use the Conditional Or operator (||) instead of the regular Or operator (|), like this:

```
if ((salesTotal < 1000.0) || (salesClass == 3))
    commissionRate = 0.0;
```

Like the Conditional And operator (&&), the Conditional Or operator stops evaluating as soon as it knows what the outcome is. Suppose that the sales total is $500. Then there's no need to evaluate the second expression. Because the first expression evaluates to true and only one of the expressions needs to be true, Java can skip the second expression. If the sales total is $5,000, of course, the second expression must be evaluated.

As with the And operators, you should use the regular Or operator only if your program depends on some side effect of the second expression, such as work done by a method call.

## Combining logical operators

You can combine simple Boolean expressions to create more complicated expressions. For example:

```
if ( (salesTotal<1000.0)||((salesTotal<5000.0) &&
        (salesClass==1))||((salesTotal < 10000.0) &&
        (salesClass == 2)))
    commissionRate = 0.0;
```

Can you tell what the expression in this if statement does? It sets the commission to zero if any one of the following three conditions is true:

>> The sales total is less than $1,000.

>> The sales total is less than $5,000, and the sales class is 1.

>> The sales total is less than $10,000, and the sales class is 2.

In many cases, you can clarify how an expression works just by indenting its pieces differently and spacing out its subexpressions. This version of the preceding if statement is a little easier to follow:

```
if (
        (salesTotal < 1000.0)
    || ( (salesTotal < 5000.0) && (salesClass == 1) )
    || ( (salesTotal < 10000.0) && (salesClass == 2) )
    )
    commissionRate = 0.0;
```

Figuring out exactly what this if statement does, however, is still tough. In many cases, the better thing to do is skip the complicated expression and code separate if statements:

```
if (salesTotal < 1000.0)
    commissionRate = 0.0;
if ((salesTotal < 5000.0) && (salesClass == 1))
    commissionRate = 0.0;
if ((salesTotal < 10000.0) && (salesClass == 2))
    commissionRate = 0.0;
```

WARNING

In Java, Boolean expressions can get a little complicated when you use more than one logical operator, especially if you mix And and Or operators. Consider this expression:

```
if ( a==1 && b==2 || c==3 )
    System.out.println("It's true!");
else
    System.out.println("No it isn't!");
```

What do you suppose this if statement does if a is 5, b is 7, and c = 3? The answer is that the expression evaluates to true, and "It's true!" is printed. That's because Java applies the operators from left to right. So the && operator is applied to a==1 (which is false) and b==2 (which is also false, but that doesn't matter because this evaluation is skipped). Thus, the && operator returns false. Then the || operator is applied to that false result and the result of c==3, which is true. Thus the entire expression returns true.

Wouldn't this expression have been clearer if you had used a set of parentheses to clarify what the expression does? Consider this example:

```java
if ( ( a==1 && b==2 ) || c==3 )
    System.out.println("It's true!");
else
    System.out.println("No it isn't!");
```

Here you can clearly see that the && operator is evaluated first.

# Using the switch Statement

In this section, you discover another Java tool for decision-making: the switch statement. The switch statement is a pretty limited beast, but it excels at making one particular type of decision: choosing one of several actions based on a value stored in an integer variable. As it turns out, the need to do just that comes up a lot. You want to keep the switch statement handy for use when such a need arises.

The basic form of the switch statement is this:

```java
switch (expression)
{
    case constant:
        statements;
        break;

    [ case constant-2:
        statements;
        break; ]...

    [ default:
        statements;
        break; ]...
}
```

The expression must evaluate to an int, short, byte, char, String, or enum. It can't be a long or a floating-point type.

You can code as many case groups as you want or need. Each group begins with the word case, followed by a constant (usually, a simple numeric or String literal) and a colon. Then you code one or more statements that you want executed if the value of the switch expression equals the constant. The last line of each case group is an optional break statement, which causes the entire switch statement to end.

The default group, which is optional, is like a catch-all case group. Its statements are executed only if none of the previous case constants match the switch expression.

**TIP**

Note that the case groups are not true blocks marked with braces. Instead, each case group begins with the case keyword and ends with the case keyword that starts the next case group. All the case groups together, however, are defined as a block marked with a set of braces.

**WARNING**

The last statement in each case group usually is a break statement. A break statement causes control to skip to the end of the switch statement. If you omit the break statement, control falls through to the next case group. Accidentally leaving out break statements is the most common cause of trouble with the switch statement.

Suppose that you need to set a commission rate based on a sales class represented by an integer (1, 2, or 3) according to this table:

| Class | Commission Rate |
|---|---|
| 1 | 2% |
| 2 | 3.5% |
| 3 | 5% |
| Any other value | 0% |

You could do this with the following `switch` statement:

```
double commissionRate;

switch (salesClass)
{
    case 1:
        commissionRate = 0.02;
        break;

    case 2:
        commissionRate = 0.035;
        break;

    case 3:
        commissionRate = 0.05;
        break;

    default:
        commissionRate = 0.0;
        break;
}
```

## Viewing an example else-if program

Many applications call for a simple logical selection of things to be done depending on some value that controls everything. As we describe earlier in this chapter, such things can be handled with big chains of `else-if` statements all strung together.

Unfortunately, these things can quickly get out of hand. `else if` chains can end up looking like DNA double-helix structures or those things that dribble down from the tops of the computer screens in *The Matrix*, with hundreds of lines of code that string `else if` after `else if`. The `switch` statement provides a much more concise alternative.

Listing 6-1 shows a bit of a program that might be used to decode error codes in a self-driving car (also known as an autonomous vehicle, or AV for short).

```java
import java.util.Scanner;

public class AVErrorDecoder1
{
    static Scanner sc = new Scanner(System.in);

    public static void main(String[] args)
    {
        System.out.println
            ("Welcome to the Autonomous Vehicle "
            + "error code decoder.\n\n"
            + "If your Autonomous Vehicle generates "
            + "an error code,\n"
            + "you can use this program to determine "
            + "the exact\ncause of the error.\n");
        System.out.print("Enter the error code: ");

        int err = sc.nextInt();

        String msg = "";
        if (err==1)
            msg = "General error.\n"
            + "Returning control to driver.";
        else if (err==2)
            msg = "System Update Required.\n"
            + "Pulling over and advising occupant "
            + "to not restart vehicle.";
        else if (err==3)
            msg = "Vehicle bored with destination.\n"
            + "Changing to something more exotic.";
        else if (err==4)
            msg = "Too many Drive Thru Windows.\n"
            + "Taking occupant to nearest health
    clinic.";
        else if (err==5)
            msg = "Dodgers game detected on audio
    system.\n"
            + "Switching to Giants.";
        else if (err==6)
```

```
            msg = "Left turn signal stuck on for more
than 10 miles.\n"
                  + "Vehicle may be too old to
drive self.";
        else if (err==7)
            msg = "Vehicle has had enough and cannot
take it anymore.\n"
                  + "Heading for nearest bridge.";
        else
            msg = "I'm sorry, Dave. I'm afraid I can't
do that.\n";

        System.out.println(msg);
    }
}
```

Wow! And this program has to decipher just 7 error codes. What if the self-driving car had 500 codes?

## Creating a better version of the example program

Fortunately, Java has a special statement that's designed just for the kind of task represented by the autonomous vehicle error decoder program: the `switch` statement. Specifically, the `switch` statement is useful when you need to select one of several alternatives based on the value of an `int`, `char`, `String`, or `enum` type variable.

TIP

An *enum* is a special kind of Java type whose value is one of several predefined constants. For example, you may have an enum named `TemperatureScale` with constant values `CELCIUS`, `FAHRENHEIT`, and `KELVIN`. A variable defined with the `TemperatureScale` type can have one of these three values.

Listing 6-2 shows a version of the self-driving car error decoder program that uses a `switch` statement instead of a big `else-if` structure. We think you'll agree that this version of the program is a bit easier to follow. The `switch` statement makes it clear that all the messages are selected based on the value of the `err` variable.

```java
import java.util.Scanner;

public class AVErrorDecoder2
{
    static Scanner sc = new Scanner(System.in);

    public static void main(String[] args)
    {
        System.out.println
            ("Welcome to the Autonomous Vehicle "
            + "error code decoder.\n\n"
            + "If your Autonomous Vehicle generates "
            + "an error code,\n"
            + "you can use this program to determine "
            + "the exact\ncause of the error.\n");
        System.out.print("Enter the error code: ");

        int err = sc.nextInt();

        String msg = "";

        switch (err)
        {
            case 1:
                msg = "General error.\n"
                    + "Returning control to driver.";
                break;
            case 2:
                msg = "System Update Required.\n"
                    + "Pulling over and advising occupant "
                    + "to not restart vehicle.";
                break;
            case 3:
                msg = "Vehicle bored with destination.\n"
                    + "Changing to something more exotic.";
                break;
            case 4:
```

```java
                msg = "Too many Drive Thru Windows.\n"
                    + "Taking occupant to nearest
health clinic.";
                break;
            case 5:
                msg = "Dodgers game detected on audio
system.\n"
                    + "Switching to Giants.";
                break;
            case 6:
                msg = "Left turn signal stuck on for
more than 10 miles.\n"
                    + "Vehicle may be too old to
drive self.";
                break;
            case 7:
                msg = "Vehicle has had enough and
cannot take it anymore.\n"
                    + "Heading for nearest bridge.";
                break;
            default:
                msg = "I'm sorry, Dave. I'm afraid
I can't do that.\n";
        }

        System.out.println(msg);
    }
}
```

**IN THIS CHAPTER**

» The thrill of while loops

» The splendor of do loops

» The wonder of for loops

# Chapter 7

# Going Around in Circles (or, Using Loops)

I n this chapter, you find out how to write programs that hang around by using *loops*, which let them execute the same statements more than once.

Loops are the key to writing one of the most common types of programs: programs that get input from the user, do something with it, get more input from the user and do something with that, and keep going this way until the user has had enough.

Put another way, loops are like the instructions on your shampoo: Lather. Rinse. *Repeat.*

## Using Your Basic while Loop

The most basic of all looping statements in Java is while. The while statement creates a type of loop that's called a *while loop*, which is simply a loop that executes continuously as long as some conditional expression evaluates to true. while loops are useful in all sorts of programming situations, so you use while loops a lot. (We tell you about other kinds of loops later in this chapter.)

## The while statement

The basic format of the while statement is this:

```
while (expression)
    statement
```

The while statement begins by evaluating the expression. If the expression is true, statement is executed. Then the expression is evaluated again, and the whole process repeats. If the expression is false, statement is not executed, and the while loop ends.

Note that the statement part of the while loop can either be a single statement or a block of statements contained in a pair of braces. Loops that have just one statement aren't very useful, so nearly all the while loops you code use a block of statements. (Well, okay, sometimes loops with a single statement are useful. It isn't unheard of — just not all that common.)

## A counting loop

Here's a simple program that uses a while loop to print the even numbers from 2 through 20 on the console:

```
public class EvenCounter
{
    public static void main(String[] args)
    {
        int number = 2;

        while (number <= 20)
        {
            System.out.print(number + " ");
            number += 2;
        }

        System.out.println();
    }
}
```

If you run this program, the following output is displayed in the console window:

```
2 4 6 8 10 12 14 16 18 20
```

The conditional expression in this program's while statement is number <= 20. That means the loop repeats as long as the value of number is less than or equal to 20. The body of the loop consists of two statements. The first prints the value of number followed by a space to separate this number from the next one. Then the second statement adds 2 to number.

# Breaking Out of a Loop

In many programs, you need to set up a loop that has some kind of escape clause. Java's escape clause is the break statement. When a break statement is executed in a while loop, the loop ends immediately. Any remaining statements in the loop are ignored, and the next statement executed is the statement that follows the loop.

Suppose that you're afraid of the number 12. (We're not doctors, and don't play ones on TV, but we think the scientific name for this condition would be *dodecaphobia*.) You could modify the counting program shown in the preceding section so that when it gets to the number 12, it panics and aborts the loop:

```java
public class Dodecaphobia
{
    public static void main(String[] args)
    {
        int number = 2;

        while (number <= 20)
        {
            if (number == 12)
                break;
            System.out.print(number + " ");
            number += 2;
        }
        System.out.println();
    }
}
```

When you run this program, the following line is displayed on the console:

```
2 4 6 8 10
```

Whew! That was close. Almost printed the number 12 there.

# Using the continue Statement

The break statement is rather harsh: It completely bails out of the loop. Sometimes that's what you need — but just as often, you don't really need to quit the loop; you just need to skip a particular iteration of the loop. The Dodecaphobia program presented earlier in this chapter stops the loop when it gets to 12. What if you just want to skip the number 12, so you go straight from 10 to 14?

To do that, you can use the break statement's kinder, gentler relative, the continue statement. The continue statement sends control right back to the top of the loop, where the expression is immediately evaluated again. If the expression is still true, the loop's statement or block is executed again.

Here's a version of the Dodecaphobia program that uses a continue statement to skip the number 12 rather than stop counting altogether when it reaches 12:

```java
public class Dodecaphobia3
{
    public static void main(String[] args)
    {
        int number = 0;

        while (number < 20)
        {
            number += 2;
            if (number == 12)
                continue;
            System.out.print(number + " ");
        }
        System.out.println();
    }
}
```

Run this program, and you get the following output in the console window:

```
2 4 6 8 10 14 16 18 20
```

Notice that we had to make several changes in this program to get it to work with a continue statement instead of a break statement. If we had just replaced the word break with continue, the program wouldn't have worked, because the statement that added 2 to the number came after the break statement in the original version. As a result, if you just replace the break statement with a continue statement, you end up with an infinite loop when you reach 12, because the statement that adds 2 to number never gets executed.

To make this program work with a continue statement, we rearranged the statements in the loop body so that the statement that adds 2 to number comes before the continue statement. That way, the only statement skipped by the continue statement is the one that prints number to the console.

Unfortunately, this change affected other statements in the program. Because 2 is added to number before number is printed, we had to change the initial value of number from 2 to 0, and we had to change the while expression from number <= 20 to number < 20.

# Running do-while Loops

A *do-while loop* (sometimes just called a *do loop*) is similar to a while loop, but with a critical difference: In a do-while loop, the condition that stops the loop isn't tested until after the statements in the loop have executed at least once. The basic form of a do-while loop is this:

```
do
    statement
while (expression);
```

Note that the while keyword and the expression aren't coded until *after* the body of the loop. As with a while loop, the body for a do-while loop can be a single statement or a block of statements enclosed in braces.

Also, notice that the expression is followed by a semicolon. `do-while` is the only looping statement that ends with a semicolon.

Here's a version of the `EvenCounter` program that uses a `do-while` loop instead of a `while` loop:

```
public class EvenCounter2
{
    public static void main(String[] args)
    {
        int number = 2;

        do
        {
            System.out.print(number + " ");
            number += 2;
        } while (number <= 20);
        System.out.println();
    }
}
```

**REMEMBER**

Here's the most important thing to remember about `do-while` loops: The statement or statements in the body of a `do-while` loop *always* get executed at least once. By contrast, the statement or statements in the body of a `while` loop aren't executed at all if the `while` expression is `false` the first time it's evaluated.

Here are a few other things to be aware of concerning `do-while` loops:

>> You often can skip initializing the variables that appear in the expression before the loop, because the expression isn't evaluated until the statements in the loop body have been executed at least once. But remember that any variables mentioned in the `while` expression must be within scope of the `do` statement itself; variables declared *within* the do loop can't be used in the `while` expression because they're out of scope.

>> You can use `break` and `continue` statements in a `do-while` loop, just as you can in a `while` loop.

>> Some programmers like to place the brace that begins the loop body on the same line as the do statement and the

while statement that ends the do-while loop on the same line as the brace that marks the end of the loop body. Whatever makes you happy is fine with us. Just remember that the compiler is agnostic when it comes to matters of indentation and spacing.

# Using the Famous for Loop

In addition to while and do-while loops, Java offers the *for loop*. You may have noticed that many loops involve counting. It turns out that counting loops are quite common in computer programs, so the people who design computer programming languages (they're called computer programming language designers) long ago concocted a special kind of looping mechanism that's designed just for counting.

The basic principle behind a typical for loop is that the loop itself maintains a *counter variable* — that is, a variable whose value increases each time the body of the loop is executed. If you want a loop that counts from 1 to 10, you'd use a counter variable that starts with a value of 1 and is increased by 1 each time through the loop. Then you'd use a test to end the loop when the counter variable passes 10. The for loop lets you set all this up in one convenient statement.

## Understanding the formal format of the for loop

We would now like to inform you of the formal format of the for loop, so that you'll know how to form it from now on. The for loop follows this basic format:

```
for (initialization-expression; test-expression; count-expression)
    statement;
```

The three expressions in the parentheses following the keyword for control how the for loop works. The following paragraphs explain what these three expressions do:

>> The *initialization expression* is executed before the loop begins. Usually, you use this expression to initialize the

counter variable. If you haven't declared the counter variable before the for statement, you can declare it here too.

>> The *test expression* is evaluated each time the loop is executed to determine whether the loop should keep looping. Usually, this expression tests the counter variable to make sure that it is still less than or equal to the value you want to count to. The loop keeps executing as long as this expression evaluates to true. When the test expression evaluates to false, the loop ends.

>> The *count expression* is evaluated each time the loop executes. Its job is usually to increment the counter variable.

Here's a simple for loop that displays the numbers 1 to 10 on the console:

```
public class CountToTen
{
    public static void main(String[] args)
    {
        for (int i = 1; i <= 10; i++)
            System.out.println(i);
    }
}
```

Run this program, and here's what you see on the console:

```
1
2
3
4
5
6
7
8
9
10
```

This for loop has the following pieces:

>> The initialization expression is int i = 1. This expression declares a variable named i of type int and assigns it an initial value of 1.

>> The test expression is i <= 10. As a result, the loop continues to execute as long as i is less than or equal to 10.

>> The count expression is i++. As a result, each time the loop executes, the variable i is incremented.

>> The body of the loop is the single statement System.out. println(i). As a result, each time the loop executes, the value of the i variable is printed to the console.

## Scoping out the counter variable

If you declare the counter variable in the initialization statement, the scope of the counter variable is limited to the for statement itself. Thus, you can use the variable in the other expressions that appear within the parentheses and in the body of the loop, but you can't use it outside the loop. This example code causes a compiler error:

```
public class CountToTenError
{
    public static void main(String[] args)
    {
        for (int i = 1; i <= 10; i++)
            System.out.println(i);
        System.out.println("The final value of i is " + i);
    }
}
```

That's because the last statement in the main method refers to the variable i, which has gone out of scope because it was declared within the for loop.

If you want to access the counter variable outside of the loop, you should declare the counter variable prior to the for statement, as in this example:

```
public class CountToTenErrorFixed
{
    public static void main(String[] args)
    {
        int i;
        for (i = 1; i <= 10; i++)
            System.out.println(i);
```

```
        System.out.println("The final value of i is " + i);
    }
}
```

Note that because the i variable is declared before the for statement, the initialization expression doesn't name the variable's data type. When you run this program, the following appears in the console window:

```
1
2
3
4
5
6
7
8
9
10
The final value of i is 11
```

## Counting even numbers

Earlier in this chapter, you saw a program that counts even numbers up to 20. You can do that with a for loop too. All you have to do is adjust the count expression. Here's a version of the CountEven program that uses a for loop:

```
public class ForEvenCounter
{
    public static void main(String[] args)
    {
        for (int number = 2; number <= 20; number += 2)
            System.out.print(number + " ");
        System.out.println();
    }
}
```

Run this program, and sure enough, the console window displays the following:

```
2 4 6 8 10 12 14 16 18 20
```

# Counting backward

No rule says for loops can only count forward. To count backward, you simply have to adjust the three for loop expressions. As usual, the initialization expression specifies the starting value for the counter variable. The test expression uses a greater-than test instead of a less-than test, and the count expression subtracts from the counter variable rather than adding to it.

For example:

```java
public class CountDown
{
    public static void main(String[] args)
    {
        for (int count = 10; count >= 1; count--)
            System.out.println(count);
    }
}
```

Run this program, and you see this result in the console window:

```
10
9
8
7
6
5
4
3
2
1
```

IN THIS CHAPTER

» Seeing some good reasons to use
methods in your programs

» Creating methods that return values

» Creating methods that accept
parameters

# Chapter **8**

# Adding Some Methods to Your Madness

n Java, a *method* is a block of statements that has a name and can be executed by *calling* (also called *invoking*) it from some other place in your program.

In this chapter, you find out how to create additional methods that are part of your application's class. Then you can call these methods from your main method. As you'll see, this technique turns out to be very useful for all but the shortest Java programs.

## The Basics of Making Methods

All methods — including the main method — must begin with a *method declaration*. Here's the basic form of a method declaration, at least for the types of methods we talk about in this chapter:

```
public static return-type method-name (parameter-list)
{
    statements...
}
```

The following paragraphs describe the method declaration piece by piece:

>> `public`: This keyword indicates that the method's existence should be publicized to the world and that any Java program that knows about your program (or, more accurately, the class defined for your Java program) should be able to use your method. That's not very meaningful for the types of programs you're dealing with at this point in the book, but it becomes more meaningful in Chapter 10: There you find out more about what `public` means and see some alternatives to `public` that are useful in various and sundry situations.

>> `static`: This keyword declares that the method is a *static method*, which means that you can call it without first creating an instance of the class in which it's defined. The `main` method must always be static.

>> `return-type`: After the word `static` comes the *return type*, which indicates whether the method returns a value when it is called and, if so, what type the value is. If the method doesn't return a value, specify `void`. (We talk more about methods that return values later in this chapter, in the section "Methods That Return Values.")

>> `method-name`: Now comes the name of your method. The rules for making up method names are the same as the rules for creating variable names: You can use any combination of letters and numbers, but the name can't start with a number. Also, it can include the dollar sign ($) and underscore character (_). No other special characters are allowed.

>> `parameter-list`: You can pass one or more values to a method by listing the values in parentheses following the method name. The parameter list in the method declaration lets Java know what types of parameters a method should expect to receive and provides names so that the statements in the method's body can access the parameters as local variables. You discover more about parameters in the section "Methods That Take Parameters," later in this chapter.

TIP

If the method doesn't accept parameters, you must still code the parentheses that surround the parameter list. You just leave the parentheses empty.

>> **Method body:** The method body consists of one or more Java statements enclosed in a set of braces. Unlike Java

statements such as `if`, `while`, and `for`, the method body requires you to use the braces even if the body consists of only one statement.

Okay, all that was a little abstract. Now, for a concrete example, we offer a version of the `Hello, World!` program in which the message is displayed not by the `main` method, but by a method named `sayHello` that's called by the `main` method:

```
public class HelloWorldMethod
{
    public static void main(String[] args)
    {
        sayHello();
    }

    public static void sayHello()
    {
        System.out.println("Hello, World!");
    }
}
```

This program is admittedly trivial, but it illustrates the basics of creating and using methods in Java. Here, the statement in the `main` method calls the `sayHello` method, which in turn displays a message on the console.

# Methods That Return Values

Some methods do some work, and then simply return when they're finished. But many methods need to return a value when they complete their work. For example, if a method's purpose is to perform a calculation, the method will likely return the result of the calculation to the calling method so that the calling method can do something with the value. You find out how to do that in the following sections.

## Declaring the method's return type

To create a method that returns a value, you simply indicate the type of the value returned by the method on the method declaration in place of the void keyword. Here's a method declaration that creates a method that returns an int value:

```
public static int getRandomNumber()
```

Here the getRandomNumber method calculates a random number and then returns the number to the caller.

The return type of a method can be any of Java's primitive return types (described in Chapter 4):

```
int
long
float
char
short
byte
double
boolean
```

Alternatively, the return type can be a *reference type*, including a class defined by the API such as String or a class you create yourself.

## Using the return statement to return the value

When you specify a return type other than void in a method declaration, the body of the method must include a return statement that specifies the value to be returned. The return statement has this form:

```
return expression;
```

The expression must evaluate to a value that's the same type as the type listed in the method declaration. In other words, if the method returns an int, the expression in the return statement must evaluate to an int.

Here's a program that uses a method that determines a random number between 1 and 10:

```
public class RandomNumber
{
```

```
    public static void main(String[] args)
    {
        int number = getRandomNumber();
        System.out.println("The number is " + number);
    }

    public static int getRandomNumber()
    {
        int num = (int)(Math.random() * 10) + 1;
        return num;
    }
}
```

In this program, the `getRandomNumber` method uses the `Math.random` method to calculate a random number from 1 to 10. (For more information about the `Math.random` method, see Chapter 5.) The `return` statement returns the random number that was calculated.

Because the `return` statement can specify an expression as well as a simple variable, we could just as easily have written the `getRandomNumber` method like this:

```
public static int getRandomNumber()
{
    return (int)(Math.random() * 10) + 1;
}
```

Here the `return` statement includes the expression that calculates the random number.

## Using a method that returns a type

You can use a method that returns a value in an assignment statement, like this:

```
int number = getRandomNumber();
```

Here the `getRandomNumber` method is called, and the value it returns is assigned to the variable `number`.

You can also use methods that return values in expressions — such as

```
int number = getRandomNumber() * 10;
```

Here the value returned by the `getRandomNumber` method is multiplied by 10, and the result is assigned to `number`.

# You gotta have a proper return statement

If a method declares a return type other than void, it *must* use a `return` statement to return a value. The compiler doesn't let you get away with a method that doesn't have a correct `return` statement.

Things can get complicated if your `return` statements are inside `if` statements. Sometimes, the compiler gets fooled and refuses to compile your program. To explain this situation, we offer the following tale of multiple attempts to solve what should be a simple programming problem.

Suppose that you want to create a random-number method that returns random numbers between 1 and 20 but never returns 12 (because you have the condition known as dodecaphobia, which — as Lucy from *Peanuts* would tell you — is the fear of the number 12). Your first thought is to just ignore the 12s, like this:

```
public static int getRandomNumber()
{
    int num = (int)(Math.random() * 20) + 1;
    if (num != 12)
        return num;
}
```

The compiler isn't fooled by your trickery here, however. It knows that if the number is 12, the `return` statement won't get executed, so it issues the message `missing return statement` and refuses to compile your program.

Your next thought is to simply substitute 11 whenever 12 comes up:

```
public static int getRandomNumber()
{
    int num = (int)(Math.random() * 20) + 1;
    if (num != 12)
        return num;
    else
        return 11;
}
```

Later that day, you realize that this solution isn't a good one because the number isn't really random anymore. One of the requirements of a good random-number generator is that any number should be as likely as any other number to come up next. But because you're changing all 12s to 11s, you've made 11 twice as likely to come up as any other number.

To fix this error, you decide to put the random-number generator in a loop that ends only when the random number is not 12:

```java
public static int getRandomNumber()
{
    int num;
    do
    {
        num = (int)(Math.random() * 20) + 1;
        if (num != 12)
            return num;
    } while (num == 12);
}
```

But the compiler refuses to compile the method again. It turns out that the compiler is smart, but not very smart. It doesn't catch the fact that the condition in the do-while loop is the opposite of the condition in the if statement, meaning that the only way out of this loop is through the return statement in the if statement. So the compiler whines missing return statement again.

After thinking about it for a while, you come up with this solution:

```java
public static int getRandomNumber()
{
    int num;
    while (true)
    {
        num = (int)(Math.random() * 20) + 1;
        if (num != 12)
            return num;
    }
}
```

Now everyone's happy. The compiler knows that the only way out of the loop is through the return statement, your dodecaphobic user doesn't have to worry about seeing the number 12, and you know that the random number isn't twice as likely to be 11 as any other number. Life is good, and you can move on to the next topic.

# Methods That Take Parameters

A *parameter* is a value that you can pass to a method. Then the method can use the parameter as though it were a local variable initialized with the value of the variable passed to it by the calling method.

Here's a method named getRandomNumber that returns a random number between 1 and 10:

```
public static int getRandomNumber()
{
    return (int)(Math.random() * 10) + 1;
}
```

This method is useful, but it would be even more useful if you could tell it the range of numbers you want the random number to fall in. It would be nice to call the method like this to get a random number between 1 and 10:

```
int number = getRandomNumber(1, 10);
```

Then, if your program needs to roll dice, you could call the same method:

```
int number = getRandomNumber(1, 6);
```

Or, to pick a random card from a deck of 52 cards, you could call it like this:

```
int number = getRandomNumber(1, 52);
```

You wouldn't have to start with 1, either. To get a random number between 50 and 100, you'd call the method like this:

```
int number = getRandomNumber(50, 100);
```

A method that accepts parameters must list the parameters in the method declaration. The parameters are placed in a *parameter list* inside the parentheses that follow the method name. For each parameter used by the method, you list the parameter type followed by the parameter name. If you need more than one parameter, you separate the parameters with commas.

Here's a version of the getRandomNumber method that accepts parameters:

```java
public static int getRandomNumber(int min, int max)
{
    return (int)(Math.random() * (max - min + 1)) + min;
}
```

Here the method uses two parameters, both of type int, named min and max. Then, within the body of the method, these parameters can be used as though they were local variables.

# Chapter **9**

# Handling Exceptions

This chapter is about what happens when Java encounters an error situation that it can't deal with. Being an object-oriented programming language, Java handles errors by using special *exception objects* that are created when an error occurs. In addition, Java has a special statement called the `try` statement that you must use to deal with exception objects. In this chapter, you find all the gory details of working with exception objects and `try` statements.

## Understanding Exceptions

An *exception* is an object that's created when an error occurs in a Java program and Java can't automatically fix the error. The exception object contains information about the type of error that occurred. The most important information — the cause of the error — is indicated by the name of the exception class used to create the exception. You usually don't have to do anything with an exception object other than figure out which one you have.

Each type of exception that can occur is represented by a different exception class. Here are some typical exceptions:

» `IllegalArgumentException`: You passed an incorrect argument to a method.

- **≫** InputMismatchException: The console input doesn't match the data type expected by a method of the Scanner class.

- **≫** ArithmeticException: You tried an illegal type of arithmetic operation, such as dividing an integer by zero.

- **≫** IOException: A method that performs I/O encountered an unrecoverable I/O error.

- **≫** ClassNotFoundException: A necessary class couldn't be found.

There are many other types of exceptions, and you find out about many of them later in this book.

You need to know a few other things about exceptions:

- **≫** When an error occurs and an exception object is created, Java is said to have *thrown an exception.* Java has a pretty good throwing arm, so the exception is always thrown right back to the statement that caused it to be created.

- **≫** When an exception happens, your program can *catch* the exception it wants to, but it doesn't have to catch the exception if it doesn't want it. Instead, it can duck and let someone else catch the exception. That someone else is the statement that called the method that's currently executing.

- **≫** If everyone ducks and the exception is never caught by the program, the program ends abruptly and displays a nasty-looking exception message on the console.

- **≫** Two basic types of exceptions in Java are checked exceptions and unchecked exceptions:

  - A *checked exception* is an exception that the compiler requires you to provide for it one way or another. If you don't, your program doesn't compile.

  - An *unchecked exception* is an exception that you can provide for, but you don't have to.

# Catching Exceptions

Whenever you use a statement that might throw an exception, you should write special code to anticipate and catch the exception. That way, your program won't crash if the exception occurs.

You catch an exception by using a `try` statement, which usually follows this general form:

```
try
{
    statements that can throw exceptions
}
catch (exception-type identifier)
{
    statements executed when exception is thrown
}
```

Here, you place the statements that might throw an exception within a *try block*. Then you catch the exception with a *catch block*.

Here are a few things to note about `try` statements:

>> You can code more than one `catch` block. That way, if the statements in the `try` block might throw more than one type of exception, you can catch each type of exception in a separate `catch` block.

>> You can catch more than one exception in a single catch block.

>> For scoping purposes, the `try` block is its own self-contained block, separate from the `catch` block. As a result, any variables you declare in the `try` block are not visible to the `catch` block. If you want them to be, declare them immediately before the `try` statement.

>> You can also code a special block (called a *finally block*) after all the `catch` blocks. For more information about coding `finally` blocks, see the section "Using a `finally` Block," later in this chapter.

>> The various exception classes in the Java API are defined in different packages. If you use an exception class that isn't defined in the standard `java.lang` package that's always available, you need to provide an `import` statement for the package that defines the exception class.

## A simple example

To illustrate how to provide for an exception, here's a program that divides two numbers and uses a try/catch statement to catch an exception if the second number turns out to be zero:

```java
public class DivideByZero
{
    public static void main(String[] args)
    {
        int a = 5;
        int b = 0; // you know this won't work!

        try
        {
            int c = a / b; // but you try it anyway
        }
        catch (ArithmeticException e)
        {
            System.out.println("Oops, you can't divide by zero.");
        }
    }
}
```

Here, the division occurs within a try block, and a catch block handles ArithmeticException. ArithmethicException is defined by java.lang, so an import statement for it isn't necessary.

When you run this program, the following is displayed on the console:

```
Oops, you can't divide by zero.
```

There's nothing else to see here. The next section shows a more complicated example, though.

## Another example

Listing 9-1 shows a simple example of a program that uses a method to get a valid integer from the user. If the user enters a value that isn't a valid integer, the catch block catches the error and forces the loop to repeat.

LISTING 9-1: **Getting a Valid Integer**

```java
import java.util.*;

public class GetInteger
{
    static Scanner sc = new Scanner(System.in);

    public static void main(String[] args)
    {
        System.out.print("Enter an integer: ");
        int i = GetAnInteger();
        System.out.println("You entered " + i);
    }

    public static int GetAnInteger()
    {
        while (true)
        {
            try
            {
                return sc.nextInt();
            }
            catch (InputMismatchException e)
            {
                sc.next();
                System.out.print("That's not "
                    + "an integer. Try again: ");
            }
        }
    }
}
```

Here the statement that gets the input from the user and returns it to the calling method is coded within the try block. If the user enters a valid integer, this statement is the only one in this method that gets executed.

If the user enters data that can't be converted to an integer, however, the nextInt method throws an InputMismatchException. Then this exception is intercepted by the catch block — which disposes of the user's incorrect input by calling the next method and then displays an error message. Then the while loop repeats.

Here's what the console might look like for a typical execution of this program:

```
Enter an integer: three
That's not an integer. Try again: 3.001
That's not an integer. Try again: 3
You entered 3
```

Here are a couple other things to note about this program:

>> The import statement specifies java.util.* to import all the classes from the java.util package. That way, the InputMismatchException class is imported.

>> The next method must be called in the catch block to dispose of the user's invalid input because the nextInt method leaves the input value in the Scanner's input stream if an InputMismatchException is thrown. If you omit the statement that calls next, the while loop keeps reading it, throws an exception, and displays an error message in an infinite loop. If you don't believe us, look at Figure 9-1. We found this error out the hard way. (The only way to make it stop is to close the console window.)

FIGURE 9-1: Why you have to call next to discard the invalid input.

# Handling Exceptions with a Preemptive Strike

The `try` statement is a useful and necessary tool in any Java programmer's arsenal. The best way to handle exceptions, however, is to prevent them from happening in the first place. That's not possible all the time, but in many cases it is. The key is to test your data before performing the operation that can lead to an exception and then skipping or bypassing the operation of the data that is problematic. (One thing we really hate is problematic data.)

For example, you can usually avoid the ArithmethicException that results from dividing integer data by zero by checking the data before performing the division:

```
if (b != 0)
    c = a / b;
```

This eliminates the need to enclose the division in a `try` block, because you know that the division by zero won't happen.

You can apply this same technique to input validation by using the `hasNextInt` method of the Scanner class. This method checks the next input value to make sure it's a valid integer. (The Scanner class calls the next input value a *token*, but that won't be on the test.) You can do this technique in several ways, and we've been encouraging you to ponder the problem since Chapter 4. Now behold the long-awaited answer: Listing 9-2 shows a version of the GetInteger method that uses a `while` loop to avoid the exception.

**LISTING 9-2:** **Another Version of the GetInteger Method**

```
import java.util.*;

public class GetInteger2
{
    static Scanner sc = new Scanner(System.in);

    public static void main(String[] args)
    {
        System.out.print("Enter an integer: ");
        int i = GetAnInteger();
        System.out.println("You entered " + i);
```

*(continued)*

LISTING 9-2:    *(continued)*

```
    }

    public static int GetAnInteger()
    {
        while (!sc.hasNextInt())
        {
            sc.next();
            System.out.print("That's not an integer.
Try again: ");
        }
        return sc.nextInt();
    }
}
```

This is a clever little bit of programming, don't you think? The conditional expression in the while statement calls the hasNextInt method of the Scanner to see whether the next value is an integer. The while loop repeats as long as this call returns false, indicating that the next value is not a valid integer. The body of the loop calls nextLine to discard the bad data and then displays an error message. The loop ends only when you know that you have good data in the input stream, so the return statement calls nextInt to parse the data to an integer and return the resulting value.

# Catching All Exceptions at Once

Java provides a catch-all exception class called Exception that all other types of exceptions are based on. (Don't worry about the details of what we mean by that. When you read Chapter 11, it makes more sense.)

If you don't want to be too specific in a catch block, you can specify Exception instead of a more specific exception class. For example:

```
try
{
    int c = a / b;
}
catch (Exception e)
{
```

```
    System.out.println("Oops, you can't divide by zero.");
}
```

In this example, the catch block specifies Exception rather than ArithmeticException.

If you have some code that might throw several types of exceptions, and you want to provide specific processing for some types but general processing for all the others, code the try statement this way:

```
try
{
    // statements that might throw several types of exceptions
}
catch (InputMismatchException e)
{
    // statements that process InputMismatchException
}
catch (IOException e)
{
    // statements that process IOException
}
catch (Exception e)
{
    // statements that process all other exception types
}
```

In this example, imagine that the code in the try block could throw an InputMismatchException, an IOException, and perhaps some other type of unanticipated exception. Here the three catch blocks provide for each of these possibilities.

If some of the exceptions to be caught require the same processing, you can combine them in a single catch clause. Just separate the exception types with a vertical bar, like this:

```
try
{
    // statements that might throw several types of exceptions
}
catch (InputMismatchException | IOException e)
{
    // statements that process InputMismatchException or IOException
}
```

```
catch (Exception e)
{
    // statements that process all other exception types
}
```

**TIP**

If you code multiple catch blocks for a single try statement, Java catches the exceptions in the order in which you list them. Therefore, if you use more than one catch block on a try statement, always list the more specific exceptions first. If you include a catch block to catch Exception, list it last.

# Using a finally Block

A finally block is a block that appears after any of the catch blocks for a statement. It's executed whether or not any exceptions are thrown by the try block or caught by any catch blocks, and it's executed if your code uses a return statement to exit early. Its purpose is to let you clean up any mess that might be left behind by the exception, such as open files or database connections.

The basic framework for a try statement with a finally block is this:

```
try
{
    statements that can throw exceptions
}
catch (exception-type identifier)
{
    statements executed when exception is thrown
}
finally
{
    statements that are executed whether or not
exceptions occur
}
```

Listing 9-3 shows a contrived but helpful example that demonstrates how to use the finally clause. In this example, a method called divideTheseNumbers tries to divide the numbers twice. If the division fails the first time (due to a divide-by-zero exception), it tries the division again. Completely irrational, we know. But persistent, like a teenager.

LISTING 9-3: **A Program That Uses a finally Clause**

```
public class CrazyWithZeros
{
    public static void main(String[] args)
    {
        try
        {
            int answer = divideTheseNumbers(5, 0);     →7
        }
        catch (Exception e)                            →9
        {
            System.out.println("Tried twice, "
                + "still didn't work!");
        }
    }

    public static int divideTheseNumbers(int a, int b) →16
    {
        int c;
        try
        {
            c = a / b;                                 →21
            System.out.println("It worked!");          →22
        }
        catch (Exception e)
        {
            System.out.println("Didn't work the
                first time.");                         →26
            c = a / b;                                 →27
            System.out.println("It worked the
                second time!");                        →28
        }
        finally
        {
            System.out.println("Better clean up
                my mess.");                            →32
        }
        System.out.println("It worked after
            all.");                                    →34
        return c;                                      →35
    }
}
```

Here's the console output for the program:

```
Didn't work the first time.
Better clean up my mess.
Tried twice, still didn't work!
```

The following paragraphs explain what's going on, step by step:

→7: The main method calls the divideTheseNumbers method, passing 5 and 0 as the parameters. You already know that this method isn't going to work.

→9: The catch clause catches any exceptions thrown by line 7.

→16: The divideTheseNumbers method divides the two numbers passed as parameters.

→21: This line is the first attempt to divide the numbers.

→22: If the first attempt succeeds, this line is executed, and the message "It worked!" is printed. Alas, the division throws an exception, so this line never gets executed.

→26: Instead, the catch clause catches the exception, and the message "Didn't work the first time." is displayed. That's the first line in the console output.

→27: The divideTheseNumbers method stubbornly tries to divide the same two numbers again. This time, no try statement is there to catch the error.

→28: Because another exception is thrown for the second division, however, this line is never executed. Thus you don't see the message "It worked the second time!" on the console. (If you do, you're in an episode of *The Twilight Zone*.)

→32: This statement in the finally clause is always executed, no matter what happens. That's where the second line in the console output came from. After the finally clause executes, the second ArithmeticException (which wasn't caught) is thrown back up to the calling method, where it is caught by line 9. That's where the last line of the console output came from.

→34: If the division did work, this line would be executed after the try block ends, and you'd see the message "It worked after all." on the console.

→35: Then the return statement would return the result of the division.

# Chapter **10**

# Making Your Own Classes

O kay, class, it's time to learn how to create your own classes.

In this chapter, you discover the basics of creating classes in Java. All Java programs use or consist of classes, so you've already seen many examples of classes. You've seen class headers such as `public class GuessingGame` and static methods such as `public static void main`. Now, in this chapter, we show you how to create programs that have more than one class.

## Declaring a Class

All classes must be defined by a *class declaration* — lines of code that provide the name for the class and the body of the class. Here's the most basic form of a class declaration:

```
[public] class ClassName {class-body}
```

The `public` keyword indicates that this class is available for use by other classes. Although it's optional, you usually include it in your class declarations. After all, the main reason you write class declarations is so other classes can create objects from the class you're defining. (Find out more about using the `public` keyword in the section "Seeing where classes live," later in this chapter.)

## Picking class names

The `ClassName` is a name that provides a name for your class. You can use any legal Java name you want to name a class, but the following three guidelines can simplify your life:

>> **Begin the class name with a capital letter.** If the class name consists of more than one word, capitalize each word: for example, `Ball`, `RetailCustomer`, and `GuessingGame`.

>> **Whenever possible, use nouns for your class names.** Classes create objects, and nouns are the words you use to identify objects. Thus most class names should be nouns.

>> **Avoid using the name of a Java API class.** No rule says that you absolutely have to, but if you create a class that has the same name as a Java API class, you have to use fully qualified names (such as `java.util.Scanner` rather than just `Scanner`) to tell your class apart from the API class with the same name.

TIP

There are thousands of Java API classes, so avoiding them all is pretty hard. But at the least, you should avoid commonly used Java class names, as well as any API classes that your application is likely to use. Creating a class named `String` or `Math`, for example, is just asking for trouble.

REMEMBER

A Java class name must, of course, conform to Java's requirements for names in general. So, the name must begin with a letter or underscore, cannot contain white space or special characters other than underscores or dollar signs, and cannot be the same as any keyword or other reserved word such as `var`, `true`, `false`, or `null`.

## Knowing what goes in the class body

The *class body* of a class is everything that goes within the braces at the end of the class declaration. The `public class ClassName` part of a class declaration takes just one line, but the body of the class declaration may take hundreds of lines (or thousands, if you get carried away).

The class body can contain the following elements:

>> **Fields:** Variable declarations define the public or private fields of a class.

>> **Methods:** Method declarations define the methods of a class.

>> **Constructors:** A *constructor* is a block of code that's similar to a method but is run to initialize an object when an instance is created. A constructor must have the same name as the class itself, and although it resembles a method, it doesn't have a return type.

>> **Initializers:** These stand-alone blocks of code are run only once, when the class is initialized. There are actually two types, called *static initializers* and *instance initializers*.

>> **Other classes and interfaces:** A class can include another class, which is then called an *inner class* or a *nested class*. Classes can also contain interfaces.

TIP

Unlike some programming languages, Java doesn't care about the order in which items appear in the class body. Still, being consistent about the order in which you place things in your classes is a good idea. That way you know where to find them. We usually code all the fields together at the start of the class, followed by constructors and then methods.

Some programmers like to place the fields at the end of the class rather than at the beginning. Whatever brings you happiness is fine with us.

REMEMBER

The fields, methods, classes, and interfaces contained within a class are called the *members* of the class. Constructors and initializers aren't considered to be members.

## Seeing where classes live

A public class must be written in a source file that has the same name as the class, with the extension java. A public class named Greeter, for example, must be placed in a file named Greeter.java.

As a result, you can't place two public classes in the same file. The following source file (named DiceGame.java) won't compile:

```
public class DiceGame
{
    public static void main(String[] args)
    {
        Dice d = new Dice();
        d.roll();
    }
}

public class Dice
{
    public void roll()
    {
        // code that rolls the dice goes here
    }
}
```

The compiler coughs up a message indicating that Dice is a public class and must be declared in a file named Dice.java.

This problem has two possible solutions. The first is to remove the public keyword from the Dice class:

```
public class DiceGame
{
    public static void main(String[] args)
    {
        Dice d = new Dice();
        d.roll();
    }
}

class Dice
{
    public void roll()
    {
        // code that rolls the dice goes here
    }
}
```

The compiler gladly accepts this program.

When you code more than one class in a single source file, Java still creates a separate class file for each class. Thus, when you compile the DiceGame.java file, the Java compiler creates two class files: DiceGame.class and Dice.class.

Removing the public keyword from a class is acceptable for relatively small programs, but its limitation is that the Dice class is available only to the classes defined within the DiceGame.java file. If you want the Dice class to be more widely available, opt for the second solution: Place it, with the public keyword, in a separate file named Dice.java.

If you're going to create an application that has several public classes, create a separate folder for the application. Then save all the class files for the application to this folder. If you keep your class files together in the same folder, the Java compiler can find them. If you place them in separate folders, you may need to adjust your ClassPath environment variable to help the compiler find the classes.

# Working with Members

The *members* of a class are the fields and methods defined in the class body. (Technically, classes and interfaces defined within a class are members too. We don't discuss them in this book, though, so you can ignore them.)

The following sections describe the basics of working with fields and methods in your classes.

## Understanding fields

A *field* is a variable that's defined in the body of a class, outside any of the class's methods. Fields are available to all the methods of a class. In addition, if the field specifies the public keyword, the field is visible outside the class. If you don't want the field to be visible outside the class, use the private keyword instead.

A field is defined the same as any other Java variable, but it can also have a modifier that specifies the visibility of the field — that is, whether other classes can access the fields of the class you're defining. For now, we'll just use two basic forms of visibility: public and private. For a more complete discussion of visibility, see the section "Understanding visibility," later in this chapter.

To create a public field that can be accessed by other classes, use the `public` modifier:

```
public int trajectory = 0;
public String name;
public Player player;
```

To create a private field, specify `private` instead of `public`:

```
private int x_position = 0;
private int y_position = 0;
private String error_message = "";
```

Fields can also be declared as `final`:

```
public final int MAX_SCORE = 1000;
```

The value of a `final` field can't be changed after it has been initialized. *Note:* Spelling `final` field names with all capital letters is customary, but not required.

## Understanding instance methods

You define methods for a class by using the same techniques that we describe in Chapter 8. To declare a method that's available to users of your class, add the `public` keyword to the method declaration:

```
public boolean isActive()
{
    return this.isActive;
}
```

To create a private method that can be used within the class but isn't visible outside the class, use the `private` keyword:

```
private void calculateLunarTrajectory()
{
    // code to get the calculated lunar trajectory
}
```

# Understanding visibility

In the preceding sections, we mention that both fields and methods can use the `public` or `private` keyword to indicate whether the field or method can be accessed from outside the class. This is called the *visibility* of the field or method.

There are actually four distinct levels of visibility you can use:

>> `private`: For fields that shouldn't be visible to any other classes — in other words, fields that are completely internal to the class.

>> `public`: For fields that should be visible to every other Java class, including classes that are outside of the current package.

>> `protected`: For fields that should be visible only to subclasses of the current class — that is, to subclasses or inner classes.

>> `package-private`: Use this visibility for fields that should be visible to any other class within the current package. (Note that there is no `package-private` keyword in Java; that's just the default visibility if you don't specify `private`, `public`, or `protected`.)

The combination of all the members that have `public` access is sometimes called the *public interface* of your class. These members are the only means that other objects have to communicate with objects created from your class. As a result, carefully consider which public fields and methods your class declares. (Again, we use the term *interface* here in a general sense, not to be confused with the specific Java feature called interface.)

The term *expose* is sometimes used to refer to the creation of public fields and methods. If a class has a public method named isActive, for example, you could say that the class exposes the isActive method. That simply means the method is available to other classes.

**WARNING**

You can use private fields and methods within a class — but not from other classes. Private fields and methods provide implementation details that may be crucial to the operation of your class but that shouldn't be exposed to the outside world. Private fields and methods are sometimes called *internal members* because they're available only from within the class.

# Using Getters and Setters

One of the basic goals of object-oriented programming is to hide the implementation details of a class inside the class while carefully controlling what aspects of the class are exposed to the outside world. This is often referred to as *encapsulation*. As a general rule, you hide as many of the details of your implementation from the outside world as you possibly can.

One way to do that is to avoid creating public fields. Instead, make your fields private. Then, selectively grant access to the data those fields contain by adding to the class special methods called *accessors*.

There are two types of accessors. A *get accessor* (also called a *getter*) is a method that retrieves a field value, whereas a set *accessor* (*setter*) is a method that sets a field value. These methods are usually named get*FieldName* and set*FieldName*, respectively. If the field is named count, for example, the getter and setter methods are named getCount and setCount.

TIP

For boolean values, it's common to use the name is*FieldName* for the getter method. For example, if a field is named Enabled, the corresponding getter method would be named isEnabled.

Here's a class that uses a private field named Health to indicate the health of a player in a game program:

```java
public class Player
{
    private int health;

    public int getHealth()
    {
        return health;
    }

    public void setHealth(int h)
    {
        health = h;
    }
}
```

Here the health field itself is declared as private, so it can't be accessed directly. Instead, it can be accessed only through the methods getHealth and setHealth.

Creating classes with accessors rather than simple public fields offers several benefits:

>> You can create a read-only property by providing a get accessor but not a set accessor. Then other classes can retrieve the property value — but can't change it.

>> Instead of storing the property value in a private field, you can calculate it each time the get accessor method is called. Suppose you have a class named Order that includes fields named unitPrice and quantityOrdered. This class might also contain a getOrderTotal method that looks like this:

```
public double getOrderTotal()
{
    return unitPrice * quantityOrdered;
}
```

Here, instead of returning the value of a class field, the get accessor calculates the value to be returned.

>> You can protect the class from bad data by validating data in a property set accessor and either ignoring invalid data or throwing an exception if invalid data is passed to the method. Suppose that you have a set accessor for an int property named Health whose value can range from 0 to 100. Here's a set accessor that prevents the Health property from being set to an incorrect value:

```
public void setHealth(int h)
{
    if (h < 0)
        health = 0;
    else if (h > 100)
        health = 100;
    else
        health = h;
}
```

Here, if the setHealth method is called with a value less than 0, health is set to 0. Likewise, if the value is greater than 100, health is set to 100.

# Creating Constructors

A *constructor* is a block of code that's called when an instance of an object is created. In many ways, a constructor is similar to a method, but a few differences exist:

>> A constructor doesn't have a return type.

>> The name of the constructor must be the same as the name of the class.

>> Unlike methods, constructors are not considered to be members of a class. (That's important only when it comes to inheritance, which is covered in Chapter 11.)

>> A constructor is called when a new instance of an object is created. In fact, it's the new keyword that calls the constructor. After creating the object, you can't call the constructor again.

Here's the basic format for coding a constructor:

```
public ClassName (parameter-list) [throws exception...]
{
    statements...
}
```

The public keyword indicates that other classes can access the constructor. That's usually what you want, although in the next chapter, you see why you might want to create a private constructor. *ClassName* must be the same as the name of the class that contains the constructor. You code the parameter list the same way that you code it for a method.

Notice also that a constructor can throw exceptions if it encounters situations that it can't recover from. (For more information about throwing exceptions, refer to Chapter 9.)

## Creating basic constructors

Probably the most common reason for coding a constructor is to provide initial values for class fields when you create the object. Suppose that you have a class named Actor that has fields named firstName and lastName. You can create a constructor for the Actor class:

```
public Actor(String first, String last)
{
    firstName = first;
    lastName = last;
}
```

Then you create an instance of the Actor class by calling this constructor:

```
Actor a = new Actor("Arnold", "Schwarzenegger");
```

A new Actor object for Arnold Schwarzenegger is created.

Like methods, constructors can be overloaded. In other words, you can provide more than one constructor for a class, provided that each constructor has a unique signature. Here's another constructor for the Actor class:

```
public Actor(String first, String last, boolean good)
{
    firstName = first;
    lastName = last;
    goodActor = good;
}
```

This constructor lets you create an Actor object with information besides the actor's name:

```
Actor a = new Actor("Arnold", "Schwarzenegger", false);
```

## Creating default constructors

We grew up watching *Dragnet*. We can still hear Joe Friday reading some thug his rights: "You have the right to an attorney during questioning. If you desire an attorney and cannot afford one, an attorney will be appointed to you free of charge."

Java constructors are like that. Every class has a right to a constructor. If you don't provide a constructor, Java appoints one for you, free of charge. This free constructor is called the *default constructor*. It doesn't accept any parameters and doesn't do anything, but it does allow your class to be instantiated.

Thus, the following two classes are identical:

```
public class Class1
{
    public Class1() { }
}

public class Class1 { }
```

In the first example, the class explicitly declares a constructor that doesn't accept any parameters and has no statements in its body. In the second example, Java creates a default constructor that works just like the constructor shown in the first example.

**WARNING**

The default constructor is *not* created if you declare any constructors for the class. As a result, if you declare a constructor that accepts parameters and still want to have an empty constructor (with no parameters and no body), you must explicitly declare an empty constructor for the class.

An example might clear this point up. The following code does *not* compile:

```
public class BadActorApp
{
    public static void main(String[] args)
    {
        Actor a = new Actor(); // error: won't compile
    }
}

class Actor
{
    private String lastName;
    private String firstName;
    private boolean goodActor;

    public Actor(String last, String first)
    {
        lastName = last;
        firstName = first;
    }

    public Actor(String last, String first, boolean good)
```

```
        {
            lastName = last;
            firstName = first;
            goodActor = good;
        }
    }
```

This program won't compile because it doesn't explicitly provide a default constructor for the Actor class; because it does provide other constructors, the default constructor isn't generated automatically.

## Calling other constructors

A constructor can call another constructor of the same class by using the special keyword this as a method call. This technique is commonly used when you have several constructors that build on one another.

Consider this class:

```
public class Actor
{
    private String lastName;
    private String firstName;
    private boolean goodActor;

    public Actor(String last, String first)
    {
        lastName = last;
        firstName = first;
    }

    public Actor(String last, String first, boolean good)
    {
        this(last, first);
        goodActor = good;
    }
}
```

Here the second constructor calls the first constructor to set the lastName and firstName fields. Then it sets the goodActor field. Writing constructors like this is helpful because it avoids the need for duplicate code.

You have a few restrictions in using the this keyword as a constructor call:

>> You can call another constructor only in the very first statement of a constructor. Thus, the following code won't compile:

```
public Actor(String last, String first, boolean good)
{
    goodActor = good;
    this(last, first); // error: won't compile
}
```

If you try to compile a class with this constructor, you get a message saying call to this must be first statement in constructor.

>> Each constructor can call only one other constructor, but you can chain constructors. If a class has three constructors, the first constructor can call the second one, which in turn calls the third one.

>> You can't create loops in which constructors call one another. Here's a class that won't compile:

```
class CrazyClass
{
    private String firstString;
    private String secondString;

    public CrazyClass(String first, String second)
    {
        this(first);
        secondString = second;
    }

    public CrazyClass(String first)
    {
        this(first, "DEFAULT"); // error: won't compile
    }
}
```

The first constructor starts by calling the second constructor, which calls the first constructor. The compiler complains that this error is a recursive constructor invocation and politely refuses to compile the class.

# Chapter **11**
# Using Subclasses
# and Inheritance

A Java class can be based on another class. Then the class becomes like a child to the parent class: It inherits all the characteristics of the parent class, good and bad. All the visible fields and methods of the parent class are passed on to the child class. The child class can use these fields or methods as they are, or it can override them to provide its own versions. In addition, the child class can add fields or methods of its own.

In this chapter, you discover how this magic works, along with the basics of creating and using Java classes that inherit other classes. You also find out a few fancy tricks that help you get the most out of inheritance.

## Introducing Inheritance

The word *inheritance* conjures up several noncomputer meanings:

» Children inherit certain characteristics from the parents.

» Children can also inherit behavior from their parents. As they say, the apple doesn't fall far from the tree.

» When someone dies, their heirs get their stuff. Some of it is good stuff, but some of it may not be.

» You can inherit rights as well as possessions. You may be a citizen of a country by virtue of being born to parents who are citizens of that country.

In Java, *inheritance* refers to a feature of object-oriented programming that lets you create classes that are derived from other classes. A class that's based on another class is said to *inherit* the other class. The class that is inherited is called the *parent class*, the *base class*, or the *superclass*. The class that does the inheriting is called the *child class*, the *derived class*, or the *subclass*.

**TIP**

The terms *subclass* and *superclass* seem to be the preferred terms among Java gurus. So if you want to look like you know what you're talking about, use these terms. Also, be aware that the term *subclass* can be used as a verb. When you create a subclass that inherits a base class, for example, you are *subclassing* the base class.

You need to know a few important things about inheritance:

» A derived class automatically takes on all the behavior and attributes of its base class. Thus, if you need to create several classes to describe types that aren't identical but have many features in common, you can create a base class that defines all the common features. Then you can create several derived classes that inherit the common features.

» A derived class can add features to the base class it inherits by defining its own methods and fields. This is one way that a derived class distinguishes itself from its base class.

» A derived class can also change the behavior provided by the base class. A base class may provide that all classes derived from it have a method named play, for example, but each class is free to provide its own implementation of the play method. In this case, any class that extends the base class can provide its own implementation of the play method.

**TIP**

» Inheritance is best used to implement *is-a-type-of* relationships. Here are a few examples: Solitaire is a type of game; a truck is a type of vehicle; an invoice is a type of transaction. In each case, a particular kind of object is a specific type of a more general category of objects.

The following sections provide more examples that help illustrate these points.

## Motorcycles, trains, and automobiles

Inheritance is often explained in terms of real-world objects such as cars and motorcycles or birds and reptiles. Consider various types of vehicles. Cars and motorcycles are two distinct types of vehicles. If you're writing software that represents vehicles, you could start by creating a class called Vehicle that would describe the features that are common to all types of vehicles, such as wheels; a driver; the ability to carry passengers; and the ability to perform actions such as driving, stopping, turning, and crashing.

A motorcycle is a type of vehicle that further refines the Vehicle class. The Motorcycle class would inherit the Vehicle class, so it would have wheels; a driver; possibly passengers; and the ability to drive, stop, turn, and crash. In addition, it would have features that differentiate it from other types of vehicles, such as two wheels and handlebars used for steering control.

A car is also a type of vehicle. The Car class would inherit the Vehicle class, so it too would have wheels; a driver (usually); possibly some passengers; and the ability to drive, stop, turn, and crash. Also, it would have some features of its own, such as four wheels, a steering wheel, seat belts and air bags, and an optional automatic transmission.

## Game play

Because you're unlikely ever to write a program that simulates cars, motorcycles, and other vehicles, take a look at a more common example: games. Suppose that you want to develop a series of board games such as Life, Sorry!, and Monopoly. Most board games have certain features in common:

>> They have a playing board with locations that players can occupy.

>> They have players that are represented by tokens.

>> The game is played by each player taking a turn, one after the other. When the game starts, it keeps going until someone wins. (If you don't believe us, ask the kids who tried to stop a game of Jumanji before someone won.)

Each specific type of game has these basic characteristics but adds features of its own. The game Life adds features such as money, insurance policies, spouses, children, and a fancy spinner in the middle of the board. Sorry! has cards that you draw to determine each move and safety zones within which other players can't attack you. Monopoly has dice that determine movement, Chance and Community Chest cards, properties, houses, hotels, and money.

If you were designing classes for these games, you might create a generic BoardGame class that defines the basic features common to all board games and then use it as the base class for classes that represent specific board games, such as LifeGame, SorryGame, and MonopolyGame.

## A businesslike example

If vehicles or games don't make the point clear enough, here's an example from the world of business. Suppose that you're designing a payroll system, and you're working on the classes that represent the employees. You realize that the payroll includes two types of employees: salaried employees and hourly employees. So you decide to create two classes, sensibly named SalariedEmployee and HourlyEmployee.

You quickly discover that most of the work done by these two classes is identical. Both types of employees have names, addresses, Social Security numbers, totals for how much they've been paid for the year, how much tax has been withheld, and so on.

The employee types also have important differences. The most obvious one is that the salaried employees have an annual salary, and the hourly employees have an hourly pay rate. Also, hourly employees have a schedule that changes week to week, and salaried employees may have a benefit plan that isn't offered to hourly employees.

Thus you decide to create three classes instead of just two. A class named Employee handles all the features that are common to both types of employees; then this class is the base class for the SalariedEmployee and HourlyEmployee classes. These classes provide the additional features that distinguish salaried employees from hourly employees.

# Inheritance hierarchies

One of the most important aspects of inheritance is that a class derived from a base class can in turn be used as the base class for another derived class. Thus you can use inheritance to form a hierarchy of classes.

You've already seen how an Employee class can be used as a base class to create two types of subclasses: a SalariedEmployee class for salaried employees and an HourlyEmployee class for hourly employees. Suppose that salaried employees fall into two categories: management and sales. Then you could use the SalariedEmployee class as the base class for two more classes: Manager and SalesPerson.

Thus, a Manager is a type of SalariedEmployee. Because a SalariedEmployee is a type of Employee, a Manager is also a type of Employee.

# Creating Subclasses

The basic procedure for creating a subclass is simple: You just use the extends keyword on the declaration for the subclass. The basic format of a class declaration for a class that inherits a base class is this:

```
public class ClassName extends BaseClass
{
    // class body goes here
}
```

Suppose that you have a class named Ball that defines a basic ball, and you want to create a subclass named BouncingBall that adds the ability to bounce:

```
public class BouncingBall extends Ball
{
    // methods and fields that add the ability to bounce to a basic
    Ball object:

    public void bounce()
    {
```

```
                // the bounce method
        }
    }
```

Here we're creating a class named BouncingBall that extends the Ball class. (*Extends* is Java's word for *inherits*.)

The subclass automatically has all the methods and fields of the class it extends. Thus, if the Ball class has fields named size and weight, the BouncingBall class has those fields too. Likewise, if the Ball class has a method named throw, the BouncingBall class gets that method too.

You need to know some important details to use inheritance properly:

>> A subclass inherits all the visible members from its base class. Constructors are *not* considered to be members, however. As a result, a subclass does *not* inherit constructors from its base class. And a subclass does not inherit members that are not visible to it (that is, private members).

>> You can *override* a method by declaring a new member with the same signature in the subclass. For more information, see the next section.

>> A special type of visibility called protected hides fields and methods from classes outside of the current package but makes them available to subclasses and other classes within the current package. For more information, see the section "Protecting Your Members," later in this chapter.

>> You can add more methods or fields with any level of visibility to a subclass. The BouncingBall class shown earlier in this section, for example, adds a public method named bounce.

# Overriding Methods

If a subclass declares a method that has the same signature as a public method of the base class, the subclass version of the method *overrides* the base class version of the method. This technique lets you modify the behavior of a base class to suit the needs of the subclass.

Suppose you have a base class named Game that has a method named play. The base class, which doesn't represent any particular game, implements this method:

```java
public class Game
{
    public void play()
    {
    }
}
```

Then you declare a class named Chess that extends the Game class but also provides an implementation for the play method:

```java
public class Chess extends Game
{
    public void play()
    {
        System.out.println("I give up. You win.");
    }
}
```

Here, when you call the play method of a Chess object, the game announces that it gives up. (We were going to provide a complete implementation of an actual chess game program for this example, but it would have made this chapter about 600 pages long. So we opted for the simpler version here.)

Note that to override a method, several conditions have to be met:

>> The class must extend the class that defines the method you want to override.

>> The method must be visible to the subclass — you can't override a private method.

>> The method in the subclass must have the same signature as the method in the base class. In other words, the name of the method, the parameter types, and the return type must be the same. (Actually, the return type can be a more specific variant of the parent method's return type. For example, you can override a method that returns a Shape with a method that returns a Circle, because Circle is a subtype of Shape. This type of override is called a *covariant return type*.)

>> The overridden method can't reduce the visibility of the method it overrides. You can increase the visibility, but you can't decrease it.

# Protecting Your Members

You're already familiar with the `public` and `private` keywords, which are used to indicate whether class members are visible outside the class or not. When you inherit a class, all the public members of the superclass are available to the subclass, but the private members aren't.

Java provides a third visibility option that's useful when you create subclasses: `protected`. A member with `protected` visibility is available to subclasses and classes in the same package, but not to classes outside of the package. Consider this example:

```
public class Ball
{
    private double weight;

    protected double getWeight()
    {
        return this.weight;
    }

    protected void setWeight(double weight)
    {
        this.weight = weight;
    }
}

public class BaseballBall extends Ball
{
    public BaseballBall()
    {
        setWeight(5.125);
    }
}
```

Here, the getWeight and setWeight methods are declared with protected access, which means that they're visible in the subclass BaseballBall. These methods aren't visible to classes that don't extend Ball, however.

# Using the this and super Keywords in Your Subclasses

The this keyword provides a way to refer to the current object instance. It's often used to distinguish between a local variable or a parameter and a class field with the same name. For example:

```
public class Ball
{
    private int velocity;
    public void setVelocity(int velocity)
    {
        this.velocity = velocity;
    }
}
```

Here the this keyword indicates that the velocity variable referred to on the left side of the assignment statement is the class field named velocity, not the parameter with the same name.

But what if you need to refer to a field or method that belongs to a base class? To do that, you use the super keyword. It works similarly to this but refers to the instance of the base class rather than the instance of the current class.

Consider these two classes:

```
public class Ball
{
    public void hit()
    {
        System.out.println("You hit it a mile!");
    }
}

class BaseballBall extends Ball
```

```
{
    public void hit()
    {
        System.out.println("You tore the cover off!");
        super.hit();
    }
}
```

Here the `hit` method in the `BaseballBall` class calls the `hit` method of its base class object. Thus, if you call the `hit` method of a `BaseballBall` object, the following two lines are displayed on the console:

```
You tore the cover off!
You hit it a mile!
```

You can also use the `super` keyword in the constructor of a subclass to explicitly call a constructor of the superclass. For more information, see the next section.

# Understanding Inheritance and Constructors

When you create an instance of a subclass, Java automatically calls the default constructor of the base class before it executes the subclass constructor. Consider the following classes:

```
public class Ball
{
    public Ball()
    {
        System.out.println(
            "Hello from the Ball constructor");
    }
}

public class BaseballBall extends Ball
{
    public BaseBall()
    {
```

```
        System.out.println(
            "Hello from the BaseballBall constructor");
    }
}
```

If you create an instance of the BaseballBall class, the following two lines are displayed on the console:

```
Hello from the Ball constructor
Hello from the BaseballBall constructor
```

If you want, you can explicitly call a base class constructor from a subclass by using the super keyword. Because Java automatically calls the parameterless constructor for you, the only reason to do this is to call a constructor of the base class that uses a parameter. Here's a version of the Ball and BaseballBall classes in which the BaseballBall constructor calls a Ball constructor that uses a parameter:

```
public class Ball
{
    private double weight;
    public Ball(double weight)
    {
        this.weight = weight;
    }
}

public class BaseballBall extends Ball
{
    public BaseballBall()
    {
        super(5.125);
    }
}
```

Here the BaseballBall constructor calls the Ball constructor to supply a default weight for the ball.

You need to obey a few rules and regulations when working with superclass constructors:

>> If you use super to call the superclass constructor, you must do so in the very first statement in the constructor.

>> If you don't explicitly call super, the compiler inserts a call to the parameterless constructor of the base class. In that case, the base class must have a parameterless constructor. If the base class doesn't have a parameterless constructor, the compiler refuses to compile the program.

>> If the superclass is itself a subclass, the constructor for its superclass is called in the same way. This continues all the way up the inheritance hierarchy until you get to the Object class, which has no superclass.

# Using the final Keyword

Java has a final keyword that serves three purposes. When you use final with a variable, it creates a constant whose value can't be changed after it has been initialized. Constants are covered in Chapter 4, so we won't describe this use of the final keyword more here. The other two uses of the final keyword are to create final methods and final classes. We describe these two uses of final in the following sections.

## Final methods

A *final method* is a method that can't be overridden by a subclass. To create a final method, you simply add the keyword final to the method declaration. For example:

```
public class SpaceShip
{
    int velocity = 0;

    public final int getVelocity()
    {
        return this.velocity;
    }
}
```

Here the method getVelocity is declared as final. Thus, any class that uses the SpaceShip class as a base class can't override the getVelocity method. If it tries, the compiler issues the error message overridden method is final.

# Final classes

A *final class* is a class that can't be used as a base class. To declare a class as final, just add the `final` keyword to the class declaration:

```
public final class BaseballBall extends Ball
{
    // members for the BaseballBall class go here
}
```

Then no one can use the `BaseballBall` class as the base class for another class.

When you declare a class to be final, all of its methods are considered to be final as well. That makes sense when you think about it. Because you can't use a final class as the base class for another class, no class can possibly be in a position to override any of the methods in the final class. Thus all the methods of a final class are final methods.

# Chapter **12**
# Using Arrays

W e could use a raise. . . .

Oh, *arrays.* Sorry.

Arrays are an important aspect of any programming language, and Java is no exception. In this chapter, you discover just about everything you need to know about using arrays. We cover run-of-the-mill one-dimensional arrays; multidimensional arrays; and two classes that are used to work with arrays, named `Array` and `Arrays`.

## Understanding Arrays

An *array* is a set of variables that is referenced by using a single variable name combined with an index number. Each item of an array is called an *element*. All the elements in an array must be of the same type. Thus the array itself has a type that specifies what kind of elements it can contain. An `int` array can contain `int` values, for example, and a `String` array can contain strings.

The index number is written after the variable name and enclosed in brackets. So if the variable name is x, you could access a specific element with an expression like x[5].

You might think that x[5] would refer to the fifth element in the array. But index numbers start with zero for the first element, so x[5] actually refers to the sixth element. This little detail is one of the chief causes of problems when working with arrays — especially if you cut your array-programming teeth in a language in which arrays are indexed from one instead of from zero. So, in Java, get used to counting from zero instead of from one.

The real power of arrays comes from the simple fact that you can use a variable or even a complete expression as an array index. So (for example) instead of coding x[5] to refer to a specific array element, you can code x[i] to refer to the element indicated by the index variable i. You see plenty of examples of index variables throughout this chapter.

Here are a few additional tidbits of array information to ponder before you get into the details of creating and using arrays:

>> Even though an array has no corresponding class file, an array is still an object. You can refer to the array object as a whole, rather than to a specific element of the array, by using the array's variable name without an index. Thus, if x[5] refers to an element of an array, x refers to the array itself.

>> An array has a fixed length that's set when the array is created. This length determines the number of elements that can be stored in the array. The maximum index value you can use with any array is one less than the array's length. Thus, if you create an array of ten elements, you can use index values from 0 to 9.

>> You can't change the length of an array after you create the array.

>> You can access the length of an array by using the length field of the array variable. x.length, for example, returns the length of the array x.

# Creating Arrays

Before you can create an array, you must declare a variable that refers to the array. This *variable declaration* should indicate the type of elements that are stored by the array followed by a set of empty brackets, like this:

```
String[] names;
```

Here a variable named names is declared. Its type is an array of String objects.

**TIP**

Both of these statements have exactly the same effect. Most Java programmers prefer to put the brackets on the type rather than on the variable name.

By itself, that statement doesn't create an array; it merely declares a variable that can refer to an array. You can actually create the array in two ways:

>> Use the new keyword followed by the array type, this time with the brackets filled in to indicate how many elements the array can hold. For example:

```
String[] names;
names = new String[10];
```

Here, an array of String objects that can hold ten strings is created. Each of the strings in this array is initialized to an empty string.

>> As with any other variable, you can combine the declaration and the creation into one statement:

```
String[] names = new String[10];
```

Here the array variable is declared and an array is created in one statement.

>> Use a special shortcut that lets you create an array and populate it with values in one swoop:

```
String[] names = {"One", "Two", "Three"};
```

**TIP**

If you don't know how many elements the array needs at compile time, you can use a variable or an expression for the array length. Here's a routine from a method that stores player names in an array of strings. It starts by asking the user how many players are on the team. Then it creates an array of the correct size:

```
System.out.print("How many players? ");
int count = sc.nextInt(); // sc is a Scanner
String[] players = new String[count];
```

# Initializing an Array

One way to initialize the values in an array is to simply assign them one by one:

```
String[] days = new String[7];
days[0] = "Sunday";
days[1] = "Monday";
days[2] = "Tuesday";
days[3] = "Wednesday";
days[4] = "Thursday";
days[5] = "Friday";
days[6] = "Saturday";
```

Java has a shorthand way to create an array and initialize it with values:

```
String[] days = { "Sunday", "Monday", "Tuesday",
                  "Wednesday", "Thursday",
                  "Friday", "Saturday" };
```

Here each element to be assigned to the array is listed in an *array initializer*. Here's an example of an array initializer for an `int` array:

```
int[] primes = { 2, 3, 5, 7, 11, 13, 17 };
```

*Note:* The length of an array created with an initializer is determined by the number of values listed in the initializer.

An alternative way to code an initializer is this:

```
int[] primes = new int[] { 2, 3, 5, 7, 11, 13, 17 };
```

To use this type of initializer, you use the new keyword followed by the array type and a set of empty brackets. Then you code the initializer.

# Using for Loops with Arrays

One of the most common ways to process an array is with a for loop. In fact, for loops were invented specifically to deal with arrays. Here's a for loop that creates an array of 100 random numbers, with values ranging from 1 to 100:

```
int[] numbers = new int[100];
for (int i = 0; i < 100; i++)
    numbers[i] = (int)(Math.random() * 100) + 1;
```

And here's a loop that fills an array of player names with strings entered by the user:

```
Scanner sc = new Scanner();
int count = 5;
String[] players = new String[count];
for (int i = 0; i < count; i++)
{
    System.out.print("Enter player name: ");
    players[i] = sc.nextLine(); // sc is a Scanner
}
```

For this example, assume that count is an int variable that holds the number of players to enter.

You can also use a for loop to print the contents of an array. For example:

```
for (int i = 0; i < count; i++)
    System.out.println(players[i]);
```

Here the elements of a String array named players are printed to the console.

The preceding example assumes that the length of the array was stored in a variable before the loop was executed. If you don't have the array length handy, you can get it from the array's length property:

```
for (int i = 0; i < players.length; i++)
    System.out.println(players[i]);
```

## Solving a homework problem with an array

Every once in a while, an array and a for loop or two can help you solve your kids' homework problems for them. One of us once helped a daughter solve a tough homework assignment for a seventh-grade math class. The problem was stated something like this:

> Bobo (these problems always had a character named Bobo in them) visits the local high school on a Saturday and finds that all the school's 1,000 lockers are neatly closed. So he starts at one end of the school and opens them all. Then he goes back to the start and closes every other locker (lockers 2, 4, 6, and so on). Then he goes back to the start and hits every third locker: If it's open, he closes it; if it's closed, he opens it. Then he hits every fourth locker, every fifth locker, and so on. He keeps doing this all weekend long, walking the hallways opening and closing lockers 1,000 times. Then he gets bored and goes home. How many of the school's 1,000 lockers are left open, and which ones are they?

Sheesh!

This problem presented a challenge, but also a great opportunity to learn about for loops and arrays. We wrote a little program that sets up an array of 1,000 Booleans. Each represents a locker: true meant open, and false meant closed. The program uses a pair of nested for loops to do the calculation.

However, the lockers are numbered 1 to 1,000, but the elements in the array are numbered 0 to 999, so that discrepancy is going to cause problems.

Our solution was to create the array with 1,001 elements and ignore the first one. That way, the indexes corresponded nicely to the locker numbers.

The finished program appears in Listing 12-1.

---

**LISTING 12-1:** **The Classic Locker Problem Solved**

```
public class BoboAndTheLockers
{
    public static void main(String[] args)
    {
        // true = open; false = closed
        boolean[] lockers = new boolean[1001];          →6

        // close all the lockers
        for (int i = 1; i <= 1000; i++)                 →9
            lockers[i] = false;
        for (int skip = 1; skip <= 1000; skip++)        →11
        {
            System.out.println("Bobo is changing every "
                + skip + " lockers.");
                for (int locker = skip; locker <= 1000;
                locker += skip)                         →15
                lockers[locker] = !lockers[locker];     →16
        }
        System.out.println("Bobo is bored"
            + " now so he's going home.");
        // count and list the open lockers
        String list = "";
        int openCount = 0;
            for (int i = 1; i <= 1000; i++)             →23
            if (lockers[i])
            {
                openCount++;
                list += i + " ";
            }
        System.out.println("Bobo left " + openCount
            + " lockers open.");
        System.out.println("The open lockers are: "
            + list);
    }
}
```

---

Here are the highlights of how this program works:

→6: This line sets up an array of Booleans with 1,001 elements. We created one more element than we needed so we could ignore element 0.

→9: This for loop closes all the lockers. This step isn't really necessary because Booleans initialize to false, but being explicit about initialization is good.

→11: Every iteration of this loop represents one complete trip through the hallways opening and closing lockers. The skip variable represents how many lockers Bobo skips on each trip. First he does every locker, then every second locker, and then every third locker. So this loop simply counts from 1 to 1,000.

→15: Every iteration of this loop represents one stop at a locker on a trip through the hallways. This third expression in the for statement (on the next line) adds the skip variable to the index variable so that Bobo can access every nth locker on each trip through the hallways.

→16: This statement uses the not operator (!) to reverse the setting of each locker. Thus, if the locker is open (true), it's set to closed (false), and vice versa.

→23: Yet another for loop spins through all the lockers and counts the ones that are open. It also adds the locker number for each open locker to the end of a string so that all the open lockers can be printed.

This program produces more than 1,000 lines of output, but only the last few lines are important. Here they are:

```
Bobo is bored now so he's going home.
Bobo left 31 lockers open.
The open lockers are: 1 4 9 16 25 36 49 64 81 100 121 144 169 196 225
    256 289 324 361 400 441 484 529 576 625 676 729 784 841 900 961
```

So, there's the answer: 31 lockers are left open.

By the way, did you notice that the lockers that were left open were the ones whose numbers are perfect squares? Or that 31 is the largest number whose square is less than 1,000?

TIP

# Using the enhanced for loop

You can often eliminate the tedium of working with indexes in for loops by using a special type of for loop called an *enhanced* for *loop*. Enhanced for loops are often called for-each loops because they automatically retrieve each element in a iterable object. Using a for-each loop eliminates the need to create and initialize an index, increment the index, test for the last item in the array, and access each array item using the index.

When it's used with an array, the enhanced for loop has this format:

```
for (type identifier : array)
{
    Statements...
}
```

The type identifies the type of the elements in the array, and the identifier provides a name for a local variable that is used to access each element. The colon operator (often read as "in") is then followed by the name of the array you want to process.

Here's an example:

```
String[] days = { "Sunday", "Monday", "Tuesday",
                  "Wednesday", "Thursday",
                  "Friday", "Saturday" };
for (String day : days)
{
    System.out.println(day);
}
```

This loop prints the following lines to the console:

```
Sunday
Monday
Tuesday
Wednesday
Thursday
Friday
Saturday
```

In other words, it prints each of the strings in the array on a separate line.

It's important to note that the for-each loop gives you a copy of each item in the array, not the item itself. So, you can't alter the contents of an array by using a for-each loop. Consider this code snippet:

```java
int[] nums = {1, 2, 3, 4, 5};

for (int n : nums)
    n = n * 2;

for (int n : nums)
    System.out.println(n);
```

You may expect this code to print the values 2, 4, 6, 8, and 10 because you multiplied n by 2 in the for-each loop. But instead, the code prints 1, 2, 3, 4, and 5. That's because n holds a copy of each array item, not the array item itself.

## Using Arrays with Methods

You can write methods that accept arrays as parameters and return arrays as return values. You just use an empty set of brackets to indicate that the parameter type or return type is an array. You've already seen this in the familiar main method declaration:

```java
public static void main(String[] args)
```

Here's a static method that creates and returns a String array with the names of the days of the week:

```java
public static String[] getDaysOfWeek()
{
    String[] days = { "Sunday", "Monday", "Tuesday",
                      "Wednesday", "Thursday",
                      "Friday", "Saturday" };
    return days;
}
```

And here's a static method that prints the contents of any String array to the console, one string per line:

```
public static void printStringArray(String[] strings)
{
    for (String s : strings)
        System.out.println(s);
}
```

Finally, here are two lines of code that call these methods:

```
String[] days = getDaysOfWeek();
printStringArray(days);
```

The first statement declares a String array and then calls getDaysOfWeek to create the array. The second statement passes the array to the printStringArray method as a parameter.

# Using Varargs

*Varargs* provides a convenient way to create a method that accepts a variable number of arguments. When you use varargs, the last argument in the method signature uses ellipses to indicate that the caller can provide one or more arguments of the given type.

Here's an example:

```
public static void PrintSomeWords(String... words)
{
    for (String word : words)
        System.out.println(word);
}
```

Here, the PrintSomeWords method specifies that the caller can pass any number of String arguments to the method (including none at all) and that the arguments will be gathered up in an array named words.

Here's a snippet of code that calls the PrintSomeWords methods using various numbers of arguments to prove the point:

```
PrintSomeWords();
```

```
PrintSomeWords("I");
PrintSomeWords("Am", "Not");
PrintSomeWords("Throwing", "Away", "My", "Shot");
```

The resulting console output looks like this:

```
I
Am
Not
Throwing
Away
My
Shot
```

An important caveat about using varargs is that the variable argument must always be the last argument in the argument list. This makes sense when you consider that, otherwise, the compiler wouldn't be able to keep track of the arguments if any other than the last argument had a variable number. So, the following won't compile:

```
public static void PrintSomeWords(String head, String... words,
    string tail)
{
}
```

You'll get a warning that says, "Varargs parameter must be the last parameter."

# Using Two-Dimensional Arrays

The elements of an array can be any type of object you want, including another array. In the latter case, you have a *two-dimensional array*, sometimes called an *array of arrays*.

Two-dimensional arrays are often used to track data in column-and-row format, much the way that a spreadsheet works. Suppose that you're working on a program that tracks five years' worth of sales (2022 through 2026) for a company, with the data broken down for each of four sales territories (North, South, East, and West). You could create 20 separate variables, with names such as `sales2022North`, `sales2022South`, `sales2022East`, and so on. But that gets a little tedious.

Alternatively, you could create an array with 20 elements, like this:

```
double[] sales = new sales[20];
```

But then how would you organize the data in this array so that you know the year and sales region for each element?

With a two-dimensional array, you can create an array with an element for each year. Each of those elements in turn is another array with an element for each region.

Thinking of a two-dimensional array as a table or spreadsheet is common, like this:

| Year | North | South | East | West |
|------|-------|-------|------|------|
| 2022 | 23,853 | 22,838 | 36,483 | 31,352 |
| 2023 | 25,483 | 22,943 | 38,274 | 33,294 |
| 2024 | 24,872 | 23,049 | 39,002 | 36,888 |
| 2025 | 28,492 | 23,784 | 42,374 | 39,573 |
| 2026 | 31,932 | 23,732 | 42,943 | 41,734 |

# Creating a two-dimensional array

To declare a two-dimensional array for this sales data, you simply list two sets of empty brackets, like this:

```
double sales[][];
```

Here `sales` is a two-dimensional array of type `double`. To put it another way, `sales` is an array of `double` arrays.

To create the array, you use the `new` keyword and provide lengths for each set of brackets, as in this example:

```
sales = new double[5][4];
```

Here the first dimension specifies that the `sales` array has five elements. This array represents the rows in the table. The second dimension specifies that each of those elements has an array of type `double` with four elements. This array represents the columns in the table.

**TIP**

A key point to grasp here is that one instance is of the first array, but a separate instance of the second array for each element is in the first array. So this statement actually creates five `double` arrays with four elements each. Then those five arrays are used as the elements for the first array.

Note that as with a one-dimensional array, you can declare and create a two-dimensional array in one statement, like this:

```
double[][] sales = new double[5][4];
```

Here the `sales` array is declared and created all in one statement.

## Accessing two-dimensional array elements

To access the elements of a two-dimensional array, you use two indexes. This statement sets the 2022 sales for the North region:

```
sales[0][0] = 23853.0;
```

As you might imagine, accessing the data in a two-dimensional array by hardcoding each index value can get tedious. No wonder `for` loops are normally used instead. The following bit of code uses a `for` loop to print the contents of the sales array to the console, separated by tabs. Each year is printed on a separate line, with the year at the beginning of the line. In addition, a line of headings for the sales regions is printed before the sales data. Here's the code:

```
NumberFormat cf = NumberFormat.getCurrencyInstance();
System.out.println("\tNorth\t\tSouth\t\tEast\t\tWest");
int year = 2022;
for (int y = 0; y < 5; y++)
{
    System.out.print(year + "\t");
    for (int region = 0; region < 4; region++)
    {
        System.out.print(cf.format(sales[y][region]));
```

```
        System.out.print("\t");
    }
    year++;
    System.out.println();
}
```

Assuming that the sales array has already been initialized, this code produces the following output on the console:

```
       North South East West
2022 $23,853.00 $22,838.00 $36,483.00 $31,352.00
2023 $25,483.00 $22,943.00 $38,274.00 $33,294.00
2024 $24,872.00 $23,049.00 $39,002.00 $36,888.00
2025 $28,492.00 $23,784.00 $42,374.00 $39,573.00
2026 $31,932.00 $23,732.00 $42,943.00 $41,734.00
```

**WARNING**

The order in which you nest the for loops that access each index in a two-dimensional array is crucial! The preceding example lists the sales for each year on a separate line, with the sales regions arranged in columns. You can print a listing with the sales for each region on a separate line, with the years arranged in columns, by reversing the order in which the for loops that index the arrays are nested:

```
for (int region = 0; region < 4; region++)
{
    for (int y = 0; y < 5; y++)
    {
        System.out.print(cf.format(sales[y][region]));
        System.out.print(" ");
    }
    System.out.println();
}
```

Here the outer loop indexes the region and the inner loop indexes the year:

```
$23,853.00 $25,483.00 $24,872.00 $28,492.00 $31,932.00
$22,838.00 $22,943.00 $23,049.00 $23,784.00 $23,732.00
$36,483.00 $38,274.00 $39,002.00 $42,374.00 $42,943.00
$31,352.00 $33,294.00 $36,888.00 $39,573.00 $41,734.00
```

# Initializing a two-dimensional array

The technique for initializing arrays by coding the array element values in curly braces works for two-dimensional arrays too. You just have to remember that each element of the main array is actually another array. So you have to nest the array initializers.

Here's an example that initializes the sales array:

```
double[][] sales =
    { {23853.0, 22838.0, 36483.0, 31352.0}, // 2022
      {25483.0, 22943.0, 38274.0, 33294.0}, // 2023
      {24872.0, 23049.0, 39002.0, 36888.0}, // 2024
      {28492.0, 23784.0, 42374.0, 39573.0}, // 2025
      {31932.0, 23732.0, 42943.0, 41734.0} }; // 2026
```

Here we added a comment to the end of each line to show the year that the line initializes. Notice that the left brace for the entire initializer is at the beginning of the second line, and the right brace that closes the entire initializer is at the end of the last line. Then the initializer for each year is contained in its own set of braces.

# Using jagged arrays

When you create an array with an expression such as new int[5][3], you're specifying that each element of the main array is actually an array of type int with three elements. Java, however, lets you create two-dimensional arrays in which the length of each element of the main array is different. This is sometimes called a *jagged array* because the array doesn't form a nice rectangle. Instead, its edges are jagged.

Suppose that you need to keep track of four teams, each consisting of two or three people. The teams are as follows:

| Team | Members |
|------|---------|
| A | Henry Blake, Johnny Mulcahy |
| B | Benjamin Pierce, John McIntyre, Jonathan Tuttle |
| C | Margaret Houlihan, Frank Burns |
| D | Max Klinger, Radar O'Reilly, Igor Straminsky |

The following code creates a jagged array for these teams:

```
String[][] teams
    = { {"Henry Blake", "Johnny Mulcahy"},
        {"Benjamin Pierce", "John McIntyre", "Jonathan Tuttle"},
        {"Margaret Houlihan", "Frank Burns"},
        {"Max Klinger", "Radar O'Reilly", "Igor Straminsky"} };
```

Here each nested array initializer indicates the number of strings for each subarray. The first subarray has two strings, the second has three strings, and so on.

You can use nested `for` loops to access the individual elements in a jagged array. For each element of the main array, you can use the `length` property to determine how many entries are in that element's subarray. For example:

```
for (int i = 0; i < teams.length; i++)
{
    for (int j = 0; j < teams[i].length; j++)
        System.out.println(teams[i][j]);
    System.out.println();
}
```

Notice that the length of each subarray is determined with the expression `teams[i].length`. This `for` loop prints one name on each line, with a blank line between teams, like this:

```
Margaret Houlihan
Frank Burns

Max Klinger
Radar O'Reilly
Igor Straminsky

Henry Blake
Johnny Mulcahy

Benjamin Pierce
John McIntyre
Jonathan Tuttle
```

If you don't want to fuss with keeping track of the indexes yourself, you can use an enhanced for loop and let Java take care of the indexes. For example:

```
for (String[] team : teams)
{
    for (String player : team)
        System.out.println(player);
    System.out.println();
}
```

Here the first enhanced for statement specifies that the type for the team variable is String[]. As a result, each cycle of this loop sets team to one of the subarrays in the main teams array. Then the second enhanced for loop accesses the individual strings in each subarray.

# Chapter **13**

# Ten Techniques for Easier Java Coding

J ava is a huge, sprawling language, and we've tried to do it justice in the previous chapters. But to really offer a complete look at Java would result in a book ten times this size, and who has the time or the patience to wade through such a tome? The goal of this book is to just give you the essentials of Java, and now we're tantalizingly close to achieving that goal. All that's left is to take you through a few techniques that will make your Java coding sessions easier and your Java programs more efficient.

## Compiling a Java Program from the Command Line

You can compile a program from a command prompt by using the javac command. Before you can do that, however, you need a program to compile. Follow these steps:

1. **Using any text editor (Notepad will do), type the following text in a file, and save it as** HelloApp.java:

```
public class HelloApp
{
```

```
    public static void main(String[] args)
    {
        System.out.println("Hello, World!");
    }
}
```

2. **Save the file in any directory you want.**

3. **Open a command prompt, use a** cd **command to change to the directory you saved the program file in, and then enter the command** javac HelloApp.java.

   This command compiles the program (javac) and creates a class file named HelloApp.class.

# Running a Java Program from the Command Line

When you successfully compile a Java program, you can run the program by typing the java command followed by the name of the class that contains the program's main method. To run the HelloApp program, for example, type this command:

```
C:\java\samples>java HelloApp
```

The program responds by displaying the message "Hello, World!".

# Casting Numeric Data

From time to time, you need to convert numeric data of one type to another. You may need to convert a double value to an integer, or vice versa. Some conversions can be done automatically; others are done using a technique called *casting*.

To cast a primitive value from one type to another, you use a *cast operator*, which is simply the name of a primitive type in parentheses placed before the value you want to cast. For example:

```
double pi = 3.1314;
int iPi;
iPi = (int) pi;
```

# Printing Data with System.out

Standard output is a stream designed to display text output onscreen. When you run a Java program under Windows, a special console window opens, and the standard output stream is connected to it. Then any text you send to standard output is displayed in that window. This stream is available to every Java program via the System.out field of the System class.

System.out is an instance of a class called PrintStream, which defines the print and println methods used to write data to the console. The only difference between the print and the println methods is that the println method adds a line-break character to the end of the output, so the output from the next call to print or println begins on a new line.

Because it doesn't start a new line, the print method is useful when you want to print two or more items on the same line. Here's an example:

```
int i = 64;
int j = 23;
System.out.print(i);
System.out.print(" and ");
System.out.println(j);
```

The console output produced by these lines is

```
64 and 23
```

# Getting Input with the JOptionPane Class

The JOptionPane class displays a simple dialog box to get text input from the user. Then you can use the parse methods of the primitive-type wrapper classes to convert the text entered by the user to the appropriate primitive type.

Although the JOptionPane class has many methods, the only one you need to use to get simple text input is the showInputDialog method. This method uses a single parameter that specifies the prompting message that's displayed in the dialog box. It returns a string value that you can then parse to the proper type.

The JOptionPane class is a part of the javax.swing package, so you need to add an import javax.swing.JOptionPane statement to the beginning of any program that uses this class.

Here's a simple program that uses the JOPtionPane class to get an integer value and display it on the console:

```java
import javax.swing.JOptionPane;
public class DialogApp
{
    public static void main(String[] args)
    {
        String s;
        s = JOptionPane.showInputDialog
        ("Enter an integer:");
        int x = Integer.parseInt(s);
        System.out.println("You entered " + x + ".");
    }
}
```

# Using the Unary Plus and Minus Operators

The unary plus (+) and minus (-) operators let you change the sign of an operand. The unary minus operator doesn't necessarily make an operand have a negative value. Instead, it changes whatever sign the operand has to start with. Thus, if the operand starts with a positive value, the unary minus operator changes it to negative. But if the operand starts with a negative value, the unary minus operator makes it positive. The following examples illustrate this point:

```java
int a = 5; // a is 5
int b = -a; // b is -5
int c = -b; // c is +5
```

# Using the Increment and Decrement Operators

One of the most common operations in computer programming is adding or subtracting 1 from a variable. Adding 1 to a variable is called *incrementing* the variable. Subtracting 1 is called *decrementing*. The traditional way to increment a variable is this:

```
a = a + 1;
```

Here the expression a + 1 is calculated, and the result is assigned to the variable a.

Java provides an easier way to do this type of calculation: the increment (++) and decrement (--) operators. Thus, to increment the variable a, you can code just this:

```
a++;
```

Note that you can use an increment or decrement operator in an assignment statement. Here's an example:

```
int a = 5;
int b = a--; // b is set to 4, a is set to 5
```

When the second statement is executed, the assignment is performed first, so b is set to 5. Then, a is decremented to 4.

# Using the Conditional Operator

Java has a special operator called the *conditional operator* that's designed to eliminate the need for if statements in certain situations. The general form for using the conditional operator is this:

```
boolean-expression ? expression-1 : expression-2
```

The Boolean expression is evaluated first. If it evaluates to true, *expression-1* is evaluated, and the result of this expression becomes the result of the whole expression. If the expression is false, *expression-2* is evaluated, and its results are used instead.

Suppose that you want to assign a value of 0 to an integer variable named salesTier if total sales are less than $10,000 and a value of 1 if the sales are $10,000 or more. You could do that with this statement:

```
int salesTier = salesTotal < 10000.0 ? 0 : 1;
```

# Comparing Strings

The correct way to test a string for a given value is to use the equals method of the String class:

```
if (answer.equals("Yes"))
    System.out.println("The answer is Yes.");
```

This method actually compares the value of the string object referenced by the variable with the string you pass as a parameter and returns a Boolean result to indicate whether the strings have the same value.

The String class has another method, equalsIgnoreCase, that's also useful for comparing strings. It compares strings but ignores case.

# Nesting Your Loops

A *nested loop* is a loop that is completely contained inside another loop. The loop that's inside is called the *inner loop,* and the loop that's outside is called the *outer loop.*

To demonstrate the basics of nesting, here's a simple little program that uses a pair of nested for loops:

```
public class NestedLoop
{
    public static void main(String[] args)
    {
        for(int x = 1; x < 10; x++)
        {
            for (int y = 1; y < 10; y++)
```

```
                    System.out.print(x + "-" + y + " ");
            System.out.println();
        }
    }
}
```

This program consists of two `for` loops. The outer loop uses x as its counter variable, and the inner loop uses y. For each execution of the outer loop, the inner loop executes 10 times and prints a line that shows the value of x and y for each pass through the inner loop. When the inner loop finishes, a call to `System.out.println` with no parameters forces a line break, thus starting a new line. Then the outer loop cycles so that the next line is printed.

When you run this program, the console displays this text:

```
1-1 1-2 1-3 1-4 1-5 1-6 1-7 1-8 1-9
2-1 2-2 2-3 2-4 2-5 2-6 2-7 2-8 2-9
3-1 3-2 3-3 3-4 3-5 3-6 3-7 3-8 3-9
4-1 4-2 4-3 4-4 4-5 4-6 4-7 4-8 4-9
5-1 5-2 5-3 5-4 5-5 5-6 5-7 5-8 5-9
6-1 6-2 6-3 6-4 6-5 6-6 6-7 6-8 6-9
7-1 7-2 7-3 7-4 7-5 7-6 7-7 7-8 7-9
8-1 8-2 8-3 8-4 8-5 8-6 8-7 8-8 8-9
9-1 9-2 9-3 9-4 9-5 9-6 9-7 9-8 9-9
```

# Index

## Symbols

# C

# P

# R

# S

# About the Authors

**Doug Lowe:** Doug has been writing computer programming books since the guys who invented Java were in high school. He's written books on COBOL, FORTRAN, ASP.NET, Visual Basic, IBM mainframe computers, midrange systems, PCs, web programming, and probably a few he's long since forgotten about. He's the author of more than 40 *For Dummies* books, including *Networking For Dummies*, 12th Edition; *Networking All-in-One For Dummies*, 8th Edition; *PowerPoint For Dummies*, Office 2021 Edition; and *Electronics All-in-One For Dummies*, 3rd Edition (all published by Wiley). He lives in that sunny all-American city Fresno, California, where the motto is "Please, Let It Rain!"

**Paul McFedries:** Paul is a technical writer who spends his days writing books just like the one you're holding in your hands. In fact, Paul has written more than 100 such books that have sold over four million copies worldwide. Paul's books include *HTML and CSS Essentials For Dummies* and *JavaScript Essentials For Dummies*. Paul invites everyone to drop by his personal website at https://paulmcfedries.com, or to follow him on X (www.x.com/paulmcf) or Facebook (www.facebook.com/PaulMcFedries).

# Dedication

**Doug:** To my beautiful wife, Kristen Gearhart.

**Paul:** To Karen, my lobster.

# Authors' Acknowledgments

Just because our names are the only ones you see on the cover, doesn't mean this book was a two-man show. Far from it. Sure, we did write this book's text and take its screenshots, but those represent only a part of what constitutes a "book." The rest of it is brought to you by the dedication and professionalism of Wiley's editing, graphics, and production teams, who toiled long and hard to turn our text and images into an actual book.

We offer our heartfelt thanks to everyone at Wiley who made this book possible, but we'd like to extend some special thank-yous to the folks we worked with directly: Executive Editor Lindsay Berg and Editor Elizabeth Kuball.

## Publisher's Acknowledgments

**Executive Editor:** Lindsay Berg

**Editor:** Elizabeth Kuball

**Proofreader:** Debbye Butler

**Production Editor:** Tamilmani Varadharaj

**Cover Design and Image:** Wiley